Journal of Our Times

150 YEARS IN THE LIFE OF GREATER LANSING

WRITTEN AND EDITED BY MARK NIXON

PRESENTED BY

Lansing State Journal

THE POWER OF KNOWING SINCE 1855

www.lsj.com

Acknowledgments

Several people contributed to "Journal of Our Times."

LSJ librarians Diana Buchanan and Pam Gawronski pored through scores of old newspaper clippings and reels of microfilm to provide timely research.

Veteran staff writers Hugh Leach and Chris Andrews shared valuable insights and recollections about the Lansing area's most recent history. Graphics designer David Schupbach's technical expertise helped keep this project on track. And LSJ copy editor Joan McKenna provided the needed polish to the text.

R.E. Olds Museum historian Dave Pfaff saved us from publishing several historical inaccuracies related to the auto industry.

Our deep thanks also go to David Votta at the Capital Area District Library, Val Berryman, Curator of History at the Michigan State University Museum, and Jim Munro, who owns a private collection of historic photos. They graciously opened their photo archives to researchers.

We are also indebted to these people for clarifying historical contradictions and outright errors: Kerry Chartkoff, state Capitol historian; Terry Denbow, Vice President of University Relations at Michigan State University; and Craig Whitford, President of the Historical Society of Greater Lansing.

The genesis of "Journal of Our Times" began more than a year ago with the LSJ's Sesquicentennial Task Force. Its members are: Michael G. Kane, Pam Jodway, Melissa Alford, Mickey Hirten, Jeri Norris, Skip Croley, Randy Markey, Mark Nixon, Pat O'Hearn, Gabe Santi, John Schneider and Nancy Morelli.

This book is also indebted to a previous book, "City in the Forest," by the late Lansing State Journal reporter and historian, Birt Darling.

And, of course, there are the photographers themselves – some of whom lived a century or more ago, and whose names are lost to the ages. We are nonetheless grateful for their anonymous contributions.

Among those photojournalists we DO know by name are the following:

Former LSJ Chief Photographers Bruce Cornelius and Norris Ingells; current LSJ Chief Photographer Greg DeRuiter, and current staff photographers Chris Holmes, Rod Sanford and Becky Shink. Over the years, their photographs have chronicled life in mid-Michigan the way nothing else could.

To all – thank you.

— Mark Nixon, September 2004

Table of Contents

INTRODUCTION 4

FOREWORD..5

CHAPTER ONE
A CAPITAL BEGINNING..7

CHAPTER TWO
'THE PEOPLE'S UNIVERSITY'.....................................23

CHAPTER THREE
A CAR IS BORN..45

CHAPTER FOUR
MAIN STREET 57

CHAPTER FIVE
PEOPLE...71

CHAPTER SIX
OUR COMMUNITIES 81

CHAPTER SEVEN
DISASTER..99

CHAPTER EIGHT
CHANGING TIMES.. 107

CHAPTER NINE
SERIOUS FUN 113

CHAPTER TEN
NEWSMAKERS 125

CHAPTER ELEVEN
LSJ, PAST & PRESENT 139

Introduction

The Lansing State Journal celebrates its sesquicentennial with a yearlong celebration in 2005. Through 150 years, 16 publishers, seven name changes, five building locations and

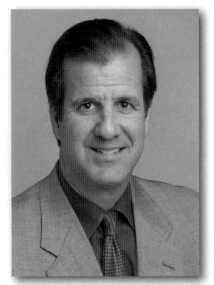

more than 45,000 editions, we've been the eyes and ears of mid-Michigan. And a remarkable community it is: capital of the great state of Michigan, home to one of the nation's great universities and birthplace of an automobile industry.

This book – "Journal of Our Times" – captures only a small bit of that fabulous history, of course. But what a story. We've mined archives throughout the region for photos that capture the vitality of our community – striking images that mark a determination to grow, innovate, prosper and, at times, overcome.

We have overcome a few obstacles of our own in producing this book. A 1951 fire in the state library (see photo, page 100) destroyed invaluable documents and photographs relevant to Greater Lansing. An employee cleaning out the LSJ library archive in 1986 mistakenly threw away microfiched news pages and photos that were rich in local history.

"Journal of Our Times" is a chronicle of the Lansing State Journal and the community it serves, both inextricably tied together ... in the past and into the future.

As we look to the future, we can certainly learn from the past. In a 1929 letter to the publisher recognizing the newspaper's 75th anniversary, President Herbert Hoover urged us to continue our "historic tradition of service to high ideals and the public good." With a new milestone now achieved, we'll continue to dedicate ourselves to doing just that.

Enjoy the "Journal of Our Times."

Michael A. Kane

Michael G. Kane
President & Publisher

Lansing State Journal
THE POWER OF KNOWING SINCE 1855
www.lsj.com

Foreword

It was a very good year, 1855. David Livingstone happened upon Victoria Falls hidden deep in the lush tropical interior of Africa; the first Daily Telegraph rolled off the presses in London, England; Henry Wadsworth Longfellow wrote the epic poem "Song of Hiawatha"; Eugene V. Debs, the impassioned U.S. labor leader, was born; Walt Whitman wrote what was perhaps his greatest tome, "Leaves of Grass"; and Michigan Agricultural College, the state's first land-grant college – now Michigan State University – was founded. Yes, history shows us that it was indeed a very good year.

There was still one more auspicious beginning in that good year. The Lansing Republican – forerunner to the Lansing State Journal – printed its first issue in a town of 1,556 that had been hewn out of densely wooded wetlands less than 10 years earlier. Literally rising from the wilderness after Lansing was made the official state capital in 1847 by the Michigan Legislature, the Lansing State Journal has been on the scene for 150 years, covering the politics, events and forces that have shaped this community and this state into the global leaders that they are today.

Founded specifically to advocate the newly formed Republican Party and to promote its agenda, The Lansing Republican also made a name for itself as an ardent proponent of abolitionism when the ugly specter of slavery loomed on the horizon of the country's newest territories.

So it has been through the Civil War, the advent of the Oldsmobile, the Great Depression, the visionary years of the civil rights movement, meetings of the Michigan Constitutional Convention, world wars, the horrific Bath School bombing – and even that most unforgettable occasion when man first stepped onto the powdery lunar surface – that the Lansing State Journal has been there to inform, enlighten, inspire, and yes, even inflame those who read her pages with their morning cup of coffee.

It is with this sesquicentennial book that we invite you to sit back, put your feet up, top off that mug and settle in for a little trip back in time. A time that may have been simpler in some respects, but when it comes right down to it, was a very restless time. A very challenging time. A time when everything was possible. And a time when people believed in those possibilities.

It is with great pride and deep respect that I offer my warmest wishes to the Lansing State Journal as it celebrates its 150th anniversary.

Governor Jennifer M. Granholm

CHAPTER ONE

A Capital Beginning

When Michigan achieved statehood in 1837, its future capital was barely more than a clearing in the woods. Lansing might have remained a backwoods afterthought if not for political horse-trading.

More than a decade after Michigan became the 26th state, legislators quartered in Detroit were still bickering about where to locate a permanent state capital. Several established cities and towns were considered. But the most unlikely place of all – a sparsely settled Lansing Township – became the ultimate choice. This was the "high, broken land" where the Grand and Red Cedar rivers joined. Not many years before, the only human inhabitants were members of the Chippewa or Ojibwa tribes. Legislators gave the future state capital a new name: Michigan.

Michigan, Michigan? The redundancy grated, so the following year yet another name change took place. The capital would be known as Lansing, in honor of a like-named community in New York state.

Land speculators and bridge builders, among others, rushed to the new state capital. The first Capitol was flung together in seven months. Cost: $22,513.02, more than twice what the Legislature had initially earmarked. It wasn't much to look at. The view from the Capitol was that of a muddy clearing. If work went past sundown, some lawmakers would carry lanterns down footpaths to reach lodgings in the business district (modern day Main Street), nearly a mile away.

Michigan's first statesmen, such as territorial governor Lewis Cass and Stevens T. Mason, the first elected governor, assured that the state would have a prominent role in the nation's westward expansion. Cass, for instance, went on to Cabinet posts in Washington and served as ambassador to France.

These early leaders created a legacy of power and influence that carried into the 21st century. People still come to Lansing to lobby, legislate and lead.

And their deeds and misdeeds are still making headlines.

◀ **Capitol cornerstone:** A stonemason sits atop the new Capitol's cornerstone in 1873 while a crowd looks on. *Courtesy Capital Area District Library*

▶ **Construction progressing:** A view of the construction's progress during the mid-1870s. The new Capitol would not be complete until late 1878. *Courtesy Capital Area District Library*

▲ **Starting from scratch:** In 1847, a decade after Michigan became the 26th state, the first Capitol was completed. Much of what became Lansing was incomplete; lawmakers leaving work after dark had to carry lanterns down muddy paths. A legislative act in 1847 changed the new capital's name from "Michigan" to Lansing. *Courtesy Capital Area District Library*

▲ **Firefighters organize:** Tom Westcott (left) poses with two companions from the Lansing Fire Department. Westcott founded the fire department in 1857 and served as one of its early chiefs. *Courtesy Capital Area District Library*

▲ **Million-dollar view:** The completed Capitol in 1879, as seen from the site of the future Lansing City Hall. The first Capitol cost more than $22,000. This new one cost nearly $1.5 million. *Courtesy Capital Area District Library*

▶ **'Boy governor':** Stevens T. Mason became Michigan's first elected governor at the ripe old age of 24. He is the youngest governor ever in U.S. history. Mason detested the "boy governor" nickname, and reputedly punched an editor who called him that. Mason served two terms as governor. Three years after leaving office in 1840, he fell ill and died. He was 31. *LSJ Archives*

THE LANSING REPUBLICAN.

BY H. BARNS.   LANSING, INGHAM CO., MICH. 1855.   VOL. L.—NO. I.

▶ **Lewis Cass:** Statesman before there was a state of Michigan, Cass was an all-important territorial governor in the decades before statehood was achieved in 1837. Cass went on to become the U.S. Secretary of War, ambassador to France and U.S. Secretary of State. *LSJ Archives*

▲ **One-horse open sleighs:** The castle-like Lansing City Hall serves as a backdrop for a winter street scene, circa 1890. *LSJ Archives*

◀ **Open for business:** About seven years after the first Capitol was dedicated, Lansing had its own weekly newspaper. Founder Henry Barns, an avowed abolitionist, printed the first edition of The Lansing Republican on April 28, 1855. A log cabin served as the first office and printing plant, located at the corner of today's Washington Avenue and Ionia Street. This front page (reprinted from our 1955 centennial edition) included news of a fatal buggy accident and reports that the Straits of Mackinac were still frozen over. *LSJ Archives*

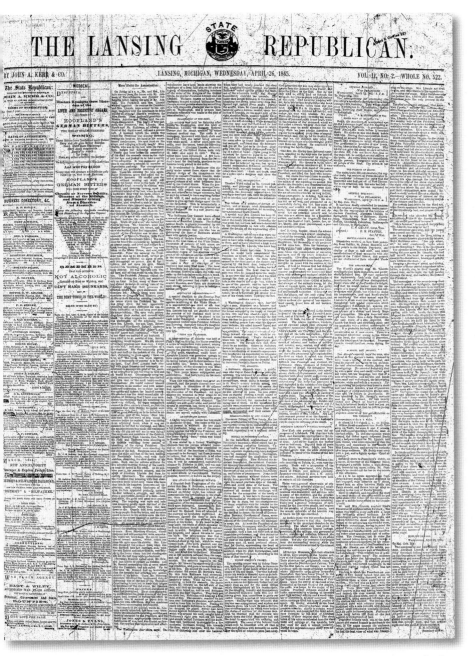

▲ ▼ **Horse power and horsepower:** Lansing's firefighting equipment was horse-drawn (above) until the 20th century. Below, what's thought to be the first motor-driven firetruck; built by the Olds Motor Works of Lansing, it was shipped to St. Louis, Mo.

Courtesy Capital Area District Library

▲ **Lincoln's assassination:** While news of President Lincoln's April 14, 1865 assassination surely reached Lansing well before this April 26th edition, the weekly newspaper devoted a great deal of space to giving details of the crime. Most of this front page is about Lincoln's death and the hunt for the assassin, John Wilkes Booth. *LSJ Archives*

▲ **Safeguarding the public:** Lansing's Board of Police and Fire Commissioners meet in 1910. Seated, from left: L.E. Imes, Clerk P.F. Gray, John Bohnet, J.E. Warner, J.P. Edmonds, and H.C. Hedges. Standing, from left: Police Chief Henry Behrendt, President E.L. Smith and Fire Chief Hugo Delfs. *Courtesy Capital Area District Library*

▶ **Capitol View:** A look down Michigan Avenue to the Capitol in 1930. *LSJ Archives*

▲ **Bridge view:** A wood-planked Michigan Avenue bridge spanned the Grand River and brought travelers to within two blocks of the relatively new Capitol. Photo, late 19th century. *Courtesy MSU Museum History Division, 7018.6.9*

▶ **Firefighting advances:** Old and modern firefighting equipment were displayed in front of the Central Fire Station in 1925. Far left: The first hand pumper used in firefighting. Lansing bought it in 1858, and later sold it to the city of Cheboygan. J.P. Edmonds eventually purchased the pumper for $45 and presented it to the museum of the Michigan Historical Society. The men (standing) in the photo are, from left: Edmonds, L.E. Imes, Ed Smith, John Bohurt and Fire Chief Hugo Delfs.

Courtesy Capital Area District Library

▲ **In remembrance:** As a memorial to the area war veterans, the city built the Lansing Civic Center (west of the Capitol) in 1954. The Civic Center fell into disrepair and was razed in 1999. Taking its place is a state office building, Constitution Hall. *LSJ Archives*

◀ **Inauguration day:** The Capitol lawn was packed when G. Mennen Williams was inaugurated governor in January 1955. *LSJ Archives*

▶ **Steady gaze:** The statue of Gov. Austin Blair gazes eastward from the Capitol lawn down Michigan Avenue. Blair was Michigan's governor throughout most of the Civil War, and was a fervent opponent of slavery. Blair is the only person to be honored with a statue on the Capitol grounds. Blair's hand rests on a Civil War battle flag. *LSJ Archives*

▲ **Growing government:** Looking west, this 1967 aerial view of the Capitol shows new complexes of state office buildings completed or under construction.
LSJ Archives

◀ **They liked Ike:** Former President Dwight D. Eisenhower addressed delegates to the Michigan Constitutional Convention on Dec. 13, 1961. "The responsibilities, best exercised by the people of a state, can be returned to them in all 50 states," Eisenhower told the Lansing Civic Center audience. "And Michigan can lead the way." The 144 delegates rewrote the state constitution, which, among other things, changed a governor's term from two years to four. *LSJ Archives*

▲ **Gov. William Milliken:** A moderate Republican, Milliken served 14 years as governor. He was known as a congenial statesman who fostered bipartisan cooperation in the Legislature. *LSJ Archives*

▲ **Republican George Romney:** A three-term governor in the 1960s, Romney fought for and eventually won passage of a state income tax. Romney was governor during the infamous Detroit riots, which he called "seven days of terror and trouble and tension."
LSJ Archives

▶ **Capitol aglow:** Lording over a modern city, the Capitol shines like a huge white beacon in 1971. *LSJ Archives*

▲ **Dignitaries:** Republican Vice President Richard Nixon stopped in Lansing in 1957 and visited Democratic Gov. G. Mennen "Soapy" Williams. Williams, famed for his bow ties, was nicknamed "Soapy" as a nod to the Mennen family, maker of soaps and toiletries. Mennen was popular with voters: He was elected six times. *LSJ Archives*

▶ **Three-term governor:** John Engler was governor for 12 years in both weak and strong economic times. Renowned for tough-minded politics, in the 1990s he spearheaded drastic cuts in property taxes, the creation of charter schools and funding public schools largely through increasing the sales tax to 6 percent. *LSJ Archives*

THE STATE JOURNAL

MICHIGAN'S COMPLETE NEWSPAPER

WEDNESDAY, APRIL 16, 1975, LANSING, MICHIGAN

PRICE—20 CENTS

Justice Swainson Took Bribe, Ex-Convict Says

John B. Swainson

By The Associated Press

John B. Swainson, a former governor and now a state Supreme Court justice, is under federal investigation for bribery based on charges made by a convicted felon.

Swainson refused to comment today on the probe.

CHIEF JUSTICE Thomas G. Kavanagh, with Swainson on his side, said today the case threatens the public's faith in the entire court.

Swainson is being investigated after convicted burglar John Whalen said he paid a $40,000 bribe to Swainson and a Detroit bondsman to ensure a Supreme Court review of Whalen's felony conviction.

Kavanagh confirmed the investigation of Swainson, but stressed the Supreme Court decision in Whalen's case was unanimous, and not decided by any single vote.

"A CHARGE such as this, even a charge made by a convicted felon, poses a threat to the court as an institution of government," said Kavanagh.

"That is why the Supreme Court, acting unanimously, sought the advice of the highly respected Albert Jenner as to how we might protect the court itself at a time when the people's faith has been shaken in some of the government's institutions."

Kavanagh said he received a telephone call early this month informing him that the U.S. Justice Department Strike Force in Detroit was looking into a bribery accusation against Swainson.

THE JUSTICES retained Jenner to represent them in the federal probe. Jenner was a former counsel for the U.S. House Judiciary Committee during its impeachment investigation, representing Republicans.

Whalen alleged $40,000 was paid to get a high court review of his conviction, which came more than two years ago in Recorder's Court.

The Supreme Court at first refused to hear the appeal but later did review the case and reversed the conviction.

Kavanagh said he does not believe the accusations against Swainson.

"WE ARE confident this matter will be resolved in a manner to maintain the peoples' confidence in the judiciary.

"After pouring over every document we could get our hands on, I just can't see that there is anything to it. But just the making of the charge against a member of the Supreme Court threatens the institution itself."

Kavanagh and Jenner plan to meet Thursday with U.S. Atty. Ralph Guy Jr. to discuss the case.

"I CAN'T think of a man in the country who we could get more liberty to find out what we want to know," the chief justice said.

THE DETROIT News said today

Cambodians Offer to Surrender

By The Associated Press

The Phnom Penh government has asked for an immediate cease-fire in its five-year war with the Khmer Rouge insurgents and offered to give up its authority, the International Committee of the Red Cross announced today in Geneva.

The offer came as the airport of Phnom Penh fell after a day of fighting and the Communist-led rebels began shelling the center of the capital.

A RED Cross spokesman said a message from Cambodia's leader, Gen. Sak Sutsakhan, was sent by telegram to Prince Norodom Sihanouk in Peking. Sihanouk, ousted from power in Cambodia in 1970, is titular leader of the insurgents.

The spokesman said it contained "a request for an immediate cease-fire and a proposal for the transfer of government powers."

Field reports in Cambodia said a massive insurgent force seized the civilian control tower at Pochentong airport four miles west of the capital in the early afternoon and by sundown had grabbed the airstrip, the rest of the airport and the military base.

The Ministry of Defense said government units were ordered to form a new defense line south of Phan Rang, which was one of two remaining government coastal enclaves.

Field reports in South Vietnam also said government troops were forced into their first retreat in the crucial battle for Xuan Loc but continued to hold the ruins of the isolated provincial capital 40 miles east of Saigon.

North Vietnamese forces captured the strategic crossroads of Dau Giay on Highway 1 about 30 miles east of Saigon.

Meanwhile, with most Americans leaving South Vietnam, Congress is considering a $200 million fund to assist in the withdrawal and to provide humanitarian aid for the Vietnamese.

The $200 million figure was agreed upon tentatively Tuesday by the Senate Foreign Relations Committee. Final decision was deferred until late today amid an indication that the panel wanted a final assurance that Americans were indeed leaving Vietnam.

DEFENSE SECRETARY James R. Schlesinger said Tuesday there were 5,850 Americans there. Last week, the total was more than 6,000. Officials say privately the total will be cut to about 1,000 within two weeks so they can be evacuated quickly in any emergency.

What a Big Chair you have, Grandma

When Bill Kelly took over the offices of the old Industrial Laundry at 1038 S. Pennsylvania for his furniture stripping business, he decided he needed a gimmick to draw attention to his endeavor. So, with scraps of wood, he constructed this giant chair which he painted red. The chair dwarfs Kelly, as he sits in it to catch up on some reading.

Staff Photo by GINGER SHARP

Keeping Courts Green Expensive

By JERRY MOSKAL
Capitol Bureau

'Where Is Spring Upturn?'

Car Sales Fail to Rally

Olds Holds Third Place

Never Mind the Dog

Tiny, Twin Pacemakers Keep Ionia Infant Alive

IN THE JOURNAL

INCREASING CLOUDINESS
Low tonight upper 30s. High Thursday upper 50s. Details Pg. A-2.

108 PAGES   8 SECTIONS
Ann Landers D-9
Ask Andy D-9
Classified .... C-6 to C-15
Comics D-9
Crossword Puzzle D-9
Deaths D-6
Earl Wilson D-9
Editorials, Columns A-10, 11
Horoscope D-9
Living Today .... D-1 to D-6
Metro News .... B-1 to B-9
Mid-Michigan B-3
News Roundup A-11
Onlooker B-1
Outdoors C-7
People in the News A-11
Sports .... C-1 to C-6
Stock Markets C-15
Theatre C-7, 8
TV Listing D-10

TELEPHONES:
HOME DELIVERY 487-6420
WANT ADS 487-6111
INFORMATION 487-6400

Journal of Our Times

▲ **Extreme makeover:** Sheathed in scaffolding, the Capitol dome gets a major face lift in 1991. The multi-year project included painstaking restoration inside the Capitol. Cost: $58.4 million. *LSJ Archives*

◀ **Scandal:** Former Gov. John B. Swainson, while a sitting Michigan Supreme Court justice, became the target of a 1975 bribery investigation. He was acquitted of a bribery charge but convicted of perjury. Swainson resigned from the court, and served 60 days in a halfway house. *LSJ Archives*

▶ **Inside the Capitol:** The dome's interior got a redo as well. Years of neglect and tacky makeovers had to be undone to restore the dome to its original splendor. The results leave visitors awestruck by the artistry and craftsmanship.

LSJ Archives

▲ **'Political universe':** In 1992, Gov. Bill Clinton, Ross Perot and President George Bush met for a historic presidential debate at MSU's Wharton Center. LSJ's front page (right) said it all: "For a time, mid-Michigan was the center of the political universe." *LSJ Archives*

SPORTS
Red Wings 5
Jets 3
Dallas Drake's two goals lead Detroit. 3D

WORLD SERIES
Blue Jays 3
Braves 2
Maldonado's 9th-inning hit wins game. 1D

TODAY
Country-powered WITL leads area radio rankings. 3C

Lansing State Journal

WEDNESDAY
October 21, 1992
35 cents

Olds denies report GM will dump division

"Those people don't understand Olds."
August Busz, Oldsmobile spokesman

Engler retreats from plan to cut senior agencies

By RICHARD S. KOONCE
Lansing State Journal

The big flag flap is over

Associated Press

■ On the campaign trail. 3A
■ C-SPAN airs student thoughts. 1B
■ Autoworkers comment about debate. 5B
■ What the media said about East Lansing. 1C

THE GREAT DEBATES

Debate is history, but not the excitement

Aftermath

Life returns to normal at MSU

For a time, mid-Michigan was the center of the political universe. People are still seeing the benefits, and could for years to come.

By KATHY BARKS HOFFMAN and GREG BOROWSKI
Lansing State Journal

President Bush and Gov. Bill Clinton greet each other before Monday night's presidential debate at MSU. Now, all that's left is the cleanup.

Lansing State Journal/DAVID OLDS

See DEBATE, Page 2A

INSIDE
Advertiser Index	2A
Ann Landers	8C
Business/Stocks	5B-8B
Classified	7D-12D
Crossword/Comics	4C
Deaths	2B
Local/State	1B-9B
Lottery	2A
Opinion	2A
Sports	1D-7D
Television	9C
Today	1C-8C

OUTSIDE
Partly cloudy today with a high expected around 50. Details, Page 2A.

TOPICS

AUTO INDUSTRY
■ Chrysler's earnings above analysts' expectations. Page 6B.

CAPITOL
■ Gov. John Engler reappoints area woman to state panel. Page 2B.

ON CAMPUS
■ Grand Valley State University's enrollment is up. Page 2B.

Poor children going hungry for lack of school breakfast

By SUZANNE WOOD
Lansing State Journal

Associated Press

Early showing, snowing by winter should fade

By SUZANNE WOOD
Lansing State Journal

CHAPTER TWO

'The People's University'

One hundred and fifty years ago, a group of men dreamed of creating a college along a tributary of the Grand River, the Red Cedar. There, hard against fields of hay and oats, young men could learn the science of agriculture.

By 1857, the first classes were held at what later became Michigan Agricultural College. It wasn't much. The student body was 63 strong. There were five people on the faculty and academic staff. The entire college comprised only three buildings.

The concept of this new college was revolutionary: Build an institution on land deeded by Congress for the express purpose of conducting research and education to benefit the public. Quite literally, MSU, the nation's original land-grant college, embodied the ideals of American democracy – of, by and for the people. What could be more directly beneficial to an agrarian nation than research and education that helped farmers put food on America's table?

As it grew, MSU mirrored how the nation itself changed. At no time did MSU change more than between World War II and the tumultuous 1960s. Not coincidentally, this was when John A. Hannah served as MSU president. During Hannah's 28-year reign, the institution went from college to university. MSU joined the Big Ten. It matured into a nationally renowned center for higher education. Student enrollment increased nearly sixfold.

Today, MSU's campus sprawls across 1,883 acres, with an adjacent 3,309 acres devoted to research. The student body is more than 44,000, making it one of the nation's largest. There are more than 200 undergraduate and graduate programs. MSU's residence hall system is the nation's biggest.

Changes from within the institution necessitated changes in the school's name; not once, but five times since 1855, when it went by the unwieldy name Agricultural College of the State of Michigan. Try working all that into a fight song!

◀ **Jubilee celebration:** MAC crowds lined up to catch a glimpse of President Theodore Roosevelt, who came to help celebrate the college's 50th anniversary in 1907. *Courtesy MSU Museum History Division, 11359-99*

▶ **On the banks of the Red Cedar:** The nation's original land-grant college, Michigan Agricultural College was deeded 676 acres to establish a campus. This is Williams Hall, circa 1870s. *Courtesy Capital Area District Library*

◄ **Botanical pioneer:** William James Beal stands before his class (background, center) in this photo, circa 1880. Beal's botanical achievements are famous. He increased corn yields by up to 50 percent; created the nation's first grass and weed garden; began the first seed-testing laboratory in the United States; and started a seed vitality experiment in 1879 that continues to this day. MSU's Beal Botanical Gardens near the university's library are named after the famous botanist. *MSU Archives*

▲ **The professor's sanctum:** Agriculture professor Herbert W. Mumford in 1896. Note the rolltop desk, strategically located close to the fireplace. *Courtesy MSU Museum History Division, 2003:152.7.16.3*

▶ **Future farmers:** All members of agriculture classes were expected to put in labor time on the campus farms or on the campus itself. Student Leslie John Smith wrote on the back of this photo: "One of my first classes, 1907, at M.A.C. taken after putting down 40' of concrete walk in front of the farm house." *Courtesy MSU Museum History Division, 2003:152.18.3*

◄ **Class in session:** This science class was held in 1897 in Linton Hall, when it was still the MAC Library and Museum. Dr. Walter B. Barrows, standing at left, was a curator of the museum and taught classes in zoology and entomology. *Courtesy MSU Museum History Division, 2000:133.1*

▲ **Jubilee celebration:** President Theodore Roosevelt gave MAC's commencement address on May 31, 1907. The year marked the college's 50th anniversary. Left: Roosevelt (back seat, left) rides through Lansing in a locally made car. *Courtesy MSU Museum History Division, 5297.1.1*

▶ **Preparing for battle:** Forerunner of the modern ROTC, Company D, MAC Cadet Corps, poses for this 1915 photo. The United States entered World War I in 1917. *Courtesy MSU Museum History Division, 1997:186.1*

▲ **Equine expert:** Ralph Hudson shows off a mare and foal near the Agriculture Building, circa 1905. In 1907, Hudson became superintendent of the Farm and Horse Department, and continued to work closely with draft horses. He became an associate professor of animal husbandry in 1930. *Courtesy MSU Museum History Division, 1998:22.22*

◀ **College postcard:** This is a view of the MAC campus, looking southeast. This postcard was mailed in 1912, showing barns where the MSU Administration Building stands today. The smokestack at left remained until the 1960s. *Courtesy MSU Museum History Division, 1998:22.82*

▲ **Those crazy freshmen:** Apparently putting up posters was an infraction of college rules. These two unfortunates, circa 1910, had to disrobe and have posters glued to their bodies. *MSU Archives*

▼ **They got game:** MAC's varsity basketball team, all seven of them, in 1910. *Courtesy MSU Museum History Division, 2000:220.1.1*

▼ **Close shave:** In 1909, a group of sophomores called Ye Vigilantes captured the freshman class president and three of his cohorts. Before being freed, the freshmen had their heads shaved – a reminder of their lowly status on campus. *Courtesy MSU Museum History Division, 5171.78.1*

▲ **Stump removal:** Students of a "land clearing short course" at MAC line up in front of a railcar that took them to farm communities for demonstrations on pulling and dynamiting tree stumps. Photo, circa 1915. *Courtesy MSU Museum History Division, 2203:152.7.26.8.1*

▲ **Party on, dudes:** By today's standards, the jerked beef party of 1911 in Wells Hall probably was pretty tame. But it was definitely out-of-bounds. Dormitory regulations stated: "Students will quietly devote themselves to study during study hours ... at no time, will rude or boisterous conduct be allowed." These students also ignored a rule about tampering with electric wiring. *Courtesy MSU Museum History Division, 4883.13.4*

▲ **Batter up!** MAC's baseball team, circa 1915. *Courtesy MSU Museum History Division, Blake Miller Family*

▲ **Coal train route:** The railroad bridge over the Red Cedar River carried train loads of coal to the campus power plant, whose smokestack can be seen on the far right. The photo was taken in 1904. *Courtesy MSU Museum History Division, 6223.2.1*

▼ **Christmas cheer:** A Christmas party at the Hesperian House in East Lansing, 1914. The Hesperian was one of several literary societies, forerunners of fraternities and sororities at MAC. *Courtesy MSU Museum History Division, Blake Miller Family*

◀ **Half-way Rock:** In the early 20th century, Half-way Rock was a familiar landmark to travelers between Lansing and East Lansing. It marked the halfway point between MAC and downtown Lansing. The boulder was split in two by a cherry tree. The tree grew from a cherry pit that someone had dropped into a small crack in the rock in the 1860s. Photo, 1913. *Courtesy MSU Museum History Division, 1998:41.11*

▲ **Ice-jammed:** Spring flooding sent tons of ice down the Red Cedar River in 1904. The ice threatened, but didn't dislodge, the railroad bridge between Wells Hall and the Engineering Building. *Courtesy MSU Museum History Division, 6223.3.5*

▲ **Campus fire:** Fire ravaged the MAC Engineering Building in March 1916. *Courtesy MSU Museum History Division, Blake Miller Family*

▲ **One building saved:** During the March 3, 1916 fire in the Engineering Building, nearby Wells Hall dormitory was evacuated. Fearing the blaze might spread to the dorm, furniture was removed and left in the snow for safekeeping. The Engineering Building was destroyed. Lansing auto pioneer R.E. Olds put up funds to rebuild the structure. *Courtesy MSU Museum History Division, 2000:220.1.1*

◀ **Going up:** The fabled Student Union Building got its start in 1923, when MAC students and faculty began digging out the basement during "Excavation Week." Men worked half days in competitive teams while female students served coffee and doughnuts. Even the Board of Trustees loaded a wagon of dirt. Lapel buttons were handed out that read, "Dig We Must." *Courtesy MSU Museum History Division, Blake Miller Family*

▲ **Campus idyll:** Farm Lane, when it really was a lane, served as a cow crossing in this photo circa 1912. *Courtesy MSU Museum History Division, Blake Miller Family*

▶ **Go team!** The 1915 MAC football team included Gideon Smith, the first African-American to play for the Aggies. MAC teams have played football since at least 1896, when the Aggies beat Lansing High School, 10-0. *Courtesy MSU Museum History Division, Blake Miller Family*

Farm helpers: The Labor Saving Caravan in 1946 was a service offered by the college's extension service. The Emergency Labor Section prepared and showed exhibits at county fairs. Exhibits included Agricultural Engineering plans and models for such things as grain elevators, buck rakes and chicken brooders. *Courtesy MSU Museum History Division, 2003:152.7.28.31*

Bovine roots: There's a reason why MAC was sometimes called "cow college." Agriculture was its stock in trade. This cheerleader rooted for the "Aggies." The nickname didn't change to Spartans until 1926. Lansing State Journal Sports Editor George Alderton is credited with giving the Aggies their new nickname. *Courtesy MSU Museum History Division, 7689-.1 (Scrapbook)*

Motor home's forerunner: Two agriculture extension specialists went on a tour in 1927 with an Upper Peninsula Home Convenience truck. All the comforts of home, including a kitchen and hot and cold running water. *Courtesy MSU Museum History Division, 2003:152.7.28.7*

Tractor class: Quite true; there were such things as tractor classes, as shown in this photo circa 1920. The device between the tractor and the sledge is a dynamometer, which measures a machine's mechanical power. *Courtesy MSU Museum History Division, 2003:152.7.18.1*

▲ **1942 polo team:** Polo was a varsity sport by the time World War II broke out. Left to right: Major Gerald Peterson, coach, Jack Burton, Norm Spatz and Fred Gibson. The players were dubbed the "Ironman Three." They were undefeated for two straight seasons. As the war dragged on, the three men graduated into the Army. *Courtesy MSU Museum History Division, 1996:183.10.2*

▲ **Big bands sound:** For decades, Band Day was a fall ritual at MSU's Spartan Stadium. Here, the East Lansing Marching Band joins 3,000 other high school musicians for a halftime show in 1985. Band Day began in 1954. MSU ended the tradition in 1992. *LSJ Archives*

▲ **12 drummers drumming:** The drumline of the MSU Marching Band, 1960. *Courtesy MSU Museum History Division*

◀ **Ready to play:** The MAC Marching Band, 1914. *Courtesy MSU Museum History Division, 2001:48.1*

▶ **Goal line to goal line:** High school bands from around Michigan take up the whole 100 yards of Spartan Stadium during the first Band Day at MSC, Nov. 6, 1954. *Courtesy MSU Museum History Division, 4946.52*

Postcard pretty: Snow and lights aglow pair up for a nighttime picture of the old Wells Hall in 1949. This second building to bear the name Wells Hall was a men's dormitory. The East Wing of the MSU Library now occupies this space, and a third Wells Hall is a classroom building across the Red Cedar River. *Courtesy MSU Museum History Division, 3638.172*

Not exactly Woodstock: Students tune in to a live outdoor concert by the MSU band in 1954. The concrete band shell was razed to make room for the construction of Bessey Hall in 1961. *Courtesy MSU Museum History Division, 5036.5.6*

More like Woodstock: Thousands of students crowded onto MSU's baseball field for a rock concert on May 24, 1970. Tie-dyed T-shirts, love beads ... you get the picture. It was the Woodstock era, and the acts were in tune with the times: Jefferson Airplane, Chicago and John Sebastian were among the headliners. *LSJ Archives*

▲ **Long sleepover:** For months during the height of a nationwide 1970 student strike on college campuses, dozens of MSU students camped out in "People's Park" near the Red Cedar River. *LSJ Archives*

▲ **Clifton Wharton:** MSU President Clifton Wharton speaks to a group of students, circa 1970. Wharton was president from 1970 to 1978. He was MSU's first minority president and the first African-American president of a major U.S. university. *LSJ Archives*

▲ **Go Green!** Captains Kent Vince and Ronald Burke hold an MSU flag during Operation Iraqi Freedom in the spring of 2003. They were providing veterinary care for military dogs. Both were ROTC members and veterinary students at MSU. *Courtesy MSU Museum History Division, 2003:173.1*

▲ **Beautiful Beaumont:** The most enduring symbol of MSU, Beaumont Tower was built in 1928. The tower and its 49 carillon bells were restored in 1995-96 at a cost of $513,000. The bells still chime regularly. *LSJ Archives*

◀ **John A. Hannah:** One of MSU's most accomplished presidents, Hannah oversaw a dramatic expansion of the campus during his tenure, 1941 to 1969. Michigan State College became Michigan State University, and enrollment soared. The student population was 7,000 in 1941. By 1969, nearly 40,000 students were enrolled. His 28-year reign was the longest in MSU history. Hannah died in 1994. *LSJ Archives*

▲ **It was the pits:** Generations of MSU students were subjected to the agonies of "The Pit," a frustrating, walk-through class registration process. Finally, technology came to the rescue. In 1992, "The Pit" was replaced with phone and computer registration. *Courtesy MSU Museum History Division, 7633.2.4*

▲ **Super-clean, superconducting:** Staff engineer Chris Compton wields a device to accelerate isotopes at MSU's National Superconducting Cyclotron Laboratory. Work on the equipment involves operating in a "clean room" to prevent outside contamination. In mid-2004, MSU was still being considered for a massive new subatomic project, the national Rare Isotope Accelerator. *LSJ Archives*

◀ **'The Barn':** Jenison Field House was affectionately known as "The Barn." It was home to decades of Spartan basketball teams, including the 1979 team that won the NCAA championship. In this January 1989 photo, the Spartans play one of their last games in Jenison. The following season was played at the new Breslin Center. *LSJ Archives*

▲ **Caught napping:** Ray Stuckey, a tuba player in the 2001 MSU Marching Band, found time for 40 winks between classes and band practice. The 300-member marching band practices a minimum of 11 hours a week – not counting individual and sectional practices – and holds a 90-minute rehearsal on game days. *LSJ Archives*

▼ **Remembering 9/11:** MSU freshman Andrew Bruck pauses to pray for the victims, and this country, a few days after the Sept. 11, 2001 terrorist attacks. *LSJ Archives*

CHAPTER THREE
A Car is Born

He lived in that wondrous time of the late 19th and early 20th centuries, the golden age of American inventors.

Thomas Edison, Henry Ford and the Wright brothers were his contemporaries. And like those pioneering geniuses, Ransom Eli Olds was a tinkerer. The Ohio-born Olds spent much of his life in Lansing; first experimenting with steam-powered vehicles in the late 1880s, then moving to the gasoline-powered "horseless carriage" in the 1890s.

By 1903, the year Orville and Wilbur Wright first mastered powered flight, an Olds-built car set a world land speed record for its weight class – nearly 60 mph.

Lansing aptly became the "Birthplace of the Oldsmobile." What is not reflected in that title is how dramatically the fortunes of one man changed the fortunes of an entire community. Lansing was thrust into the Automobile Age when Olds created the world's first progressive automotive assembly line (an idea Ford copied and automated). By 1904, the Olds Motor Works had produced more than 6,000 of the Curved Dash Runabouts.

This meant jobs, competing companies (including a second company Olds founded, the Reo Motor Car Co.), ancillary businesses, and, of course, a growing population. Will Durant, founder of General Motors, soon built his own car company in Lansing. The plant on Verlinden Street later became Fisher Body.

Now, Lansing was not only the seat of state government and a neighbor to a growing agricultural college. It was also the maker of automobiles, the lasting symbol of 20th-century American life. Ever since, the area's economy is said to stand firmly atop a three-legged stool: cars, the capital and the campus.

Times and driving tastes change. GM decided in 2000 to end the Oldsmobile line. On April 29, 2004, the last Oldsmobile rolled off the assembly line in Lansing, 117 years after R.E. Olds chugged down a Lansing street in his steam-powered car.

Life goes on.
The Oldsmobile line, unfortunately, does not.

◀ ▶ **Drive time:** In the 1870s, Lansing manufacturing leaned on its agrarian underpinnings. It was known for making farm implements, bobsleds and wheelbarrows. That began to change in the 1880s, when Ransom E. Olds began producing his version of the horseless carriage. Right: Olds shows off the second version of his steam-powered car, made in 1892. Left: An 1897, gasoline-powered version. It's widely considered to be the first Oldsmobile. *Courtesy Capital Area District Library*

▲ **Putting it together:** Olds is considered the creator of the progressive automobile assembly line. Henry Ford was a friend of Olds, and adapted Olds' ideas when Ford developed his automated assembly line in Detroit. In this 1901 photo, workers take a break from engine assembly for the famous Curved Dash Runabout. *LSJ Archives*

▶ **Showing off:** Auto pioneers like Olds had to convince the public that their products were roadworthy. Here, Olds coaxes his 1902 Curved Dash Runabout up a hill. The Curved Dash was the first mass-produced car in America. It had a 66-inch wheelbase, weighed just 650 pounds and was powered by a one-cylinder, 4-horsepower engine. Price: $650. *LSJ Archives*

▼ **Parade of cars:** Newfangled contraptions are always a hit at parades. This 1903 photo shows a parade of Curved Dash Runabouts. The Lansing parade is believed to be the first automobile parade ever. *Courtesy Capital Area District Library*

▲ **Race day:** Racing was a common way to promote car sales, even in the auto's early days. This 1903 Olds Pirate set a world land speed record for its weight class — nearly 60 mph. *LSJ Archives*

▲ **Thanks a million:** Worker and dignitaries were on hand in 1935 to cheer the 1 millionth Oldsmobile to be built. *LSJ Archives*

◀ **Wealth and fame:** The success of Olds' company brought him riches. At the wheel of a experimental Reo car, the auto pioneer poses with his family in front of their Lansing mansion, circa 1905. The mansion was designed by renowned architect Darius Moon. It had nine bedrooms, three fireplaces and a turntable on the garage floor so the driver didn't have to back out. In 1966, the mansion was razed as part of the construction of Interstate 496 — a controversy that still rankles historians and preservationists.

Courtesy Jim Munro collection

▲ **Hot work:** Shirtless workers are shown "wet sanding" the paint coat of Oldsmobile bodies, circa 1920. *LSJ Archives*

◀ **Beyond Oldsmobile:** Lansing had other, smaller automobile competitors in the early part of the 20th century. This is a bus with a Studebaker chassis and a body made by the Auto Body Company of Lansing. Circa 1920. *Courtesy Jim Munro collection*

◄ ▲ **Another auto giant:** Will Durant, founder of General Motors, began a car company in Lansing in 1920. Durant – often called "Billy" – was not an inventor like Olds. However, Durant excelled at business organization. He founded the Buick Motor Car Co. in 1905, followed by GM in 1908. Facing page and above: Durant and Star automobiles being assembled in the Lansing plant in 1921. Left: The plant on Verlinden Street, which later became GM's Fisher Body plant. Today, the facility is part of GM's Lansing Car Assembly Plant.

Courtesy Jim Munro collection

Trucks, too: R.E. Olds also started the Reo Motor Car Co., maker of cars and trucks from 1905 to 1975. The Diamond Reo truck (a 1967 model shown here) was considered among the best in the trucking world. *LSJ Archives*

Reo rolls again: Reo enthusiasts celebrated the vehicle's 100th anniversary in 2004 with a parade along South Washington Avenue. Reo – taken from Olds' initials – began as the Reo Motor Car Co., which Olds founded in the early 1900s. *LSJ Archives*

Outward bound: Lansing-made DiamondT trucks, circa 1965, are loaded on flatcars and ready to be shipped.

Courtesy Jim Munro collection

30 million and counting: In December 1989, United Auto Workers (left to right) Jerry Earls, John Butler and Dave Brace welcome the 30 millionth Oldsmobile to roll off the assembly line. *LSJ Archives*

◀ **Reo's end:** It was a sad day for Reo workers when they left work for the last time in 1975. The company went bankrupt. The plant and the famed Reo Club House were razed. *LSJ Archives*

▶ **New beginning:** The June 21, 2000 edition of the LSJ hails the groundbreaking for General Motors' $800 million car assembly plant in Delta Township. The plant will employ about 2,500 people and will be set to begin producing vehicles in 2006.

LSJ Archives

■ **Family:** Teen parents can find options, help. Page 1D

Lansing State Journal

www.lansingstatejournal.com

Sunny High near 80. Page 8B

50¢

Wednesday June 21, 2000

"We understand that we have won a very significant prize."
— Lansing Mayor David Hollister

LANSING [GM] MICHIGAN
The next step in our future.

"My next goal: a third new assembly facility."
— Art Baker, UAW Local 652 negotiator

Dream realized

GM's Delta plant lifts Lansing into new league

By Andy Henion
Lansing State Journal

Higher gas prices lead to probe

FTC investigation seeks reasons for spike to $2 a gallon

By H. Josef Hebert
Associated Press

Winners
1,642 local voters tell us what they like best about the Lansing area for the annual Best of the Best section. Inside

ROAD TRIP

Baseball wanderings
Take a look at life in the minor leagues as the Lugnuts hit the trail.
Sports/Page 1C

Report: U.S. health care ranks 37th worldwide
Associated Press

Digging in: Doug Taylor (left) of UAW Local 602, Delta Township Supervisor Joe Drolett, Lansing Mayor David Hollister, Gov. John Engler and General Motors Vice President Jerry Elson celebrate the groundbreaking Tuesday.

GM's new Delta Township plant

Bill could cut yearly phone cost by $40

State Senate OKs legislation dropping $3.28 local charge

By Paul Egan
Lansing State Journal

Township braces for changes new plant will bring

By Tim Martin
Lansing State Journal

Changing landscape: General Motors Corp.'s new plant will locate in this area in Delta Township. The township will improve roads, build more neighborhoods and likely boost its retail base as a result of the $1 billion GM complex.

HOME DELIVERY: 1-800-234-1719

◄◄ **Going down:** Oldsmobile's sign was removed in 1985 as General Motors consolidated Buick, Oldsmobile and Cadillac under one name, B-O-C. GM later moved Oldsmobile Division's headquarters to Detroit. It was a harbinger of more bad news. *LSJ Archives*

◄ **End of the line:** The last Oldsmobile to be built comes off the assembly line on April 29, 2004. Workers signed their names under the hood of the 2004 Olds Alero GLS Sedan. The last Oldsmobile (and the first one) are on display at the R.E. Olds Museum in Lansing.

LSJ Archives

CHAPTER FOUR

Main Street

Stop awhile on any mid-Michigan main street, and you'll hear murmurs of the past. The street names tell of long-ago settlers: Okemos, Chandler, Townsend, Seymour, Turner ...

True, the buildings on these streets have changed dramatically over a century and more. But the past isn't entirely blotted out. Sturdy yet graceful architecture adorns the older buildings; pieces of time that have been spared the wrecking ball.

These are our links to Main Street of the late 19th and early 20th centuries – a time when small towns like Eaton Rapids boasted hotels; when streetcars rumbled past dry good stores, corner grocers and wheelbarrow factories.

Watching the Main Streets of our communities change over the years was to watch America change. Thriving downtowns suddenly began to look seedy and outdated as they struggled to compete with suburban shopping centers and malls. The venerable downtown department store became a dinosaur.

Then – slowly, painfully – downtowns large and small began a process of rebirth. In places like Lansing's Old Town and smaller communities like Grand Ledge, folksy boutiques, bookstores and cafes are making a go of it. The so-called "urban pioneers" of the new millennium are reviving the has-beens of a different era.

And let's not forget the survivors of those bygone days. Kositchek's men's store in downtown Lansing, once located in Eaton Rapids, is more than 100 years old. Linn and Owen Jewelers has been in business since the 1920s. And that cramped little downtown landmark, the Peanut Shop, has been roasting away since 1948.

Main Street, past, present and future: Stop and gaze awhile. You'll see it all.

◀ **Busy town:** A street scene in Eaton Rapids, 1870. In the late 19th century, Eaton Rapids was a mecca for health-conscious tourists who came to bathe in the town's mineral waters. *LSJ Archives*

▶ **Before there were cars ...** There were liveries that acted as latter-day garages and "filling stations" for horses. Jimmie's Feed Barn and Livery operated in Lansing in the late 1800s. *LSJ Archives*

▲ **River city:** This overview of downtown Lansing was probably taken around the turn of the 20th century. Note the covered bridge (right foreground) crossing the Grand River. *LSJ Archives*

◀ **Eat at Brown's:** Brown's Restaurant, located on South Washington Avenue, was one of several restaurants to spring up in Lansing in the late 1800s. In this photo, circa 1891, the woman on the left is identified Mrs. James Brown – presumably the restaurant's proprietress. *LSJ Archives*

▶ **Under construction:** The Michigan Avenue bridge is under construction in this photo, circa 1893. The bridge, completed in 1895, linked a vital transportation artery between Lansing and Michigan Agricultural College. *Courtesy Capital Area District Library*

▶ **Nuts and bolts:** Hardware stores were commonplace in large towns and small. Frank Stahl (middle) was the owner of Lansing's F. Stahl Hardware in the late 1800s. *LSJ Archives*

▼ **Downtown, circa late 1870s:** This view of Washington Avenue looks north from Michigan Avenue. *Courtesy MSU Museum History Division, 7018.6.8*

◀ ▲ **Opera, anyone?** Lansing did indeed have an opera house in the late 1800s. Buck's Opera House (later to be named Baird's Opera House) was located at the corner of Washington Avenue and Ottawa Street. This was Lansing's finest location for live theater and stage shows. Things changed in 1910. Competition from movie theaters caused the owners to renovate the opera house and rename it the Gladmer Theater. The Gladmer showed a mix of live theatrical productions and silent movies.

Courtesy MSU Museum History Division, 7018.6.10 & 7018.6.5

View from a bridge: This 1895 photograph, taken from the east end of the Michigan Avenue Bridge, looks westward. The buildings in the foreground are gone. Today, there's a city park (closest to the bridge) and, directly north, the decommissioned Ottawa Power Station. *Courtesy Capital Area District Library*

Modern lamplighters: An early store of the W.F. Bohnet Electric Co., 327 N. Washington Ave., circa 1910-1920. The man in the background, left, is believed to be the owner, a Mr. Bohnet. *Courtesy MSU Museum History Division, 2924.2*

▲ **Pre-supermarket:** The corner grocer was the precursor of the giant supermarkets of today. This photo shows an unidentified grocery store, circa 1910. *MSU Archives*

◀ **Engine makers:** R.E. Olds wasn't the only one tinkering with gasoline engines. Here, workers at the Bates & Edmonds. Co., a gas engine-making firm, pose for a photo. Circa early 1900s. *LSJ Archives*

▲ **Whistle stop:** The Michigan Central Depot in Bath, 1910. *LSJ Archives*

▶ **Turn-of-the-century town:** A view of Bath's main street in 1905. Note the street's unpaved condition. *LSJ Archives*

◄ **Boomtown:** Lansing shows off its industrial vigor in this city view near Cedar and Shiawassee streets, 1910. Fueled by – among other things, auto manufacturing – Lansing's population thrived. In 1860, just 17,000 people lived in all of Ingham County. Fifty years later, Lansing's population itself exceeded 31,000. The 1920 Census put Lansing's population at more than 57,000. *LSJ Archives*

▼ **First hospital:** While there were convalescent homes and sanitariums after the Civil War, Sparrow Hospital became Lansing's first major hospital. Fund-raising began in the early 1900s, and a hospital association was established in 1903. In 1912, Edward E. Sparrow donated $100,000 to start a hospital on East Michigan Avenue. This photo was taken circa 1912. *LSJ Archives*

▲ **Roaring '20s:** A view of Abbott Road, East Lansing, in 1925. Until 1907, East Lansing was known as Collegeville. *MSU Archives*

▲ **Rutted avenue:** Though the Automobile Age was in full bloom, Lansing's Washington Avenue remained unpaved in this photo, circa 1920. Note the streetcar, which was a favored mode of transportation in the early 20th century. *LSJ Archives*

▲ **Bird's-eye view:** An aerial survey airplane maps the terrain for Abrams Aerial Survey Corp., circa 1940. The company was started by aviation pioneer and Lansing resident Talbert "Ted" Abrams. Abrams is considered the father of aerial photography. The company later built the navigation system for the lunar rover on NASA's Apollo moon missions. *LSJ Archives*

◄ **Night on the town:** Two servicemen relax with their dates at the Coral Gables Night Club in 1944. East Lansing was a "dry town" until 1968. Coral Gables was one of the closest bars for thirsty MSU students. MSC veterinary student Betsy Wright, at right with her date, Roy, wrote on the photo: "Don and Mary were married one week ago tonight and were celebrating the anniversary. Ron and Don were on leave of absence from their military duties. What a swell time we had." *Courtesy MSU Museum History Division, 5049.12.2*

▶ **The icemen cometh:** In the days before electric refrigerators, iceboxes kept perishables cool. And ice delivery trucks were a common sight – as was this one, circa 1922. *Courtesy Jim Munro collection*

▲ **Downtown Mason:** A view of Mason's Jefferson Street, circa 1940. Note the brick-paved street.

Courtesy Jim Munro collection

◀ **If it fits:** A Federal Department Store customer is measured for alterations in 1955. The store was part of Frandor Shopping Center. Frandor opened in the 1950s and is thought to be one of the nation's first shopping centers. *LSJ Archives*

▶ **Knapp's:** The art deco exterior of Knapp's Department Store, downtown Lansing, is considered one of the city's landmarks. Knapp's closed in 1981, and became offices for state workers. This photo was taken in February 1956. *LSJ Archives*

◄ **Steel Hotel:** St. Johns' Steel Hotel, photographed in 1975. Fire later destroyed the historic downtown structure. *LSJ Archives*

▼ **'The Gut':** Washington Avenue was nicknamed "The Gut" sometime in the 1950s. And "Cruising the Gut" was a popular pastime for Lansing teenagers. This photo, looking north from Washtenaw Street, was taken in 1961 at the height of "The Gut's" popularity. *LSJ Archives*

The end: Bowing to mall theaters and cineplexes, downtown theaters like East Lansing's State Theatre began to close in the 1970s and 1980s. The State's last picture show was in 1984. Soon thereafter, a few residents got front row seats as the theater was razed. Far right: Lansing's Gladmer Theatre is torn down in 1984. *LSJ Archives*

▶ **Molletes, anyone?** Pedro Lopez makes a Mexican sweetbread called molletes at Lansing's Lopez Bakery in 2001. In the 1990s, the area's Hispanic population grew by about 25 percent. *LSJ Archives*

▲ **Signing off:** The former Michigan National Tower officially lost its name in 2001 when the sign came down, symbolizing a change in ownership. As of mid-2004, the office building – tallest in downtown Lansing – had yet to have a new name. *LSJ Archives*

▼ **Link to the past:** One of Lansing's treasures, the Turner-Dodge House on Lansing's north side, remains a gathering place for festivals and holiday events. Built in 1858, the Classical Revival-style mansion was first owned by Lansing merchant James Turner. Later, son-in-law Frank L. Dodge bought and enlarged it. The house is listed on the National Register of Historic Places. *LSJ Archives*

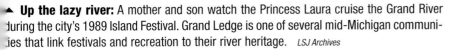

▲ **Up the lazy river:** A mother and son watch the Princess Laura cruise the Grand River during the city's 1989 Island Festival. Grand Ledge is one of several mid-Michigan communities that link festivals and recreation to their river heritage. *LSJ Archives*

CHAPTER FIVE

People

Ah, those faces.

Famous ones known the world over. Faces known only to friends and family.

Faces lined with grief or creased with laughter. Faces enthralled by victory, or sunken in despair.

Human faces. Human stories.

Whether it's the leathery visage of an aging Indian warrior like Chief Okemos, or the contented look of a mom snuggling with her newborn quads, the faces of mid-Michigan write their own poignant chapters.

The photos in this chapter are but a sampling in that unending book titled "Life in Mid-Michigan."

We chose some obvious ones: A war hero. A movie star. America's most famous civil rights leader. A Michigan statesman and renowned author. A blind singer whose songs have sold millions. Some of them once lived here. Others were just passing through.

Then there are the portraits of regular folks who happened to be in a certain place at a certain time. An LSJ photographer was there. The shutter snapped open for a split second ... and another frame of the human experience revealed itself in the daily Lansing State Journal.

◄ **'First triplets':** The population of the governor's mansion increased by three in November 1994 when triplets were born to Gov. John Engler and wife Michelle. This 2000 photo shows the proud parents holding (from left) Maggie, Hannah and Madeleine, age 5. *LSJ Archives*

▶ **String along:** Young musician Celine Seguin, 6, intently watches her teacher during a 2002 winter strings concert at MSU's Community Music School. *LSJ Archives*

◀ **Chief Okemos:** Believed to have been born in 1775, the Indian chief fought white settlers as a young warrior. Reputedly related to the great Indian warrior Chief Pontiac, Okemos later signed a peace treaty with Lewis Cass, Michigan's territorial governor. Okemos lived his entire life in mid-Michigan, often camping along the Grand River. Two area roads and a Lansing suburb bear his name. Okemos died in 1858.   *LSJ Archives*

◀ **Head librarian:** Harriet Tenney was one of Michigan's early state librarians. The photo is believed to have been taken in the late 1880s.

Courtesy Capital Area District Library

▶ **Biggie:** A Spartan legend, Clarence "Biggie" Munn was a head football coach and athletic director at MSU. He coached from 1947-53, compiling a 54-9-2 record with a consensus national championship in 1952. This photo was taken in 1954. Munn died in 1975. *LSJ Archives*

▲ **Peace marcher and president:** One of MSU's most popular faculty members, economics professor Walter Adams flashes the "peace sign" while leading a 1969 march down Michigan Avenue to the state Capitol. He's accompanied on his right by state Rep. Jackie Vaughn III. When longtime president John Hannah stepped down in 1969, Adams agreed to be temporary president during those tumultuous times. His condition: He could return to being a professor, which he considered the highest post in the university. He served for about a year, then returned to the classroom. *LSJ Archives*

▲ **Adams' trademarks:** MSU economics professor Walter Adams poses in a 1989 photo, just weeks before he retired. The cigar and bow tie were his trademarks. *LSJ Archives*

◀ **Before Martha Stewart ...** There was Martha Dixon. Dixon hosted the locally popular cooking show "Copper Kettle" from 1955 to 1976 on WJIM-TV (now WLNS-TV). This photo was taken in 1961. *LSJ Archives*

◀ **Painful memories:** The horrors of the Sept. 11, 2001 terrorist attacks revived painful memories for Bennie Allen of DeWitt. In 2002, he told a State Journal reporter about serving on the USS Thatcher, a World War II destroyer attacked twice by kamikaze pilots. Behind him are the medals and ribbons he earned. He was only 19 when the war ended. *LSJ Archives*

▶ **War hero:** Oscar Johnson, a soft-spoken DeWitt man, was one of 163 World War II veterans awarded the Medal of Honor. In Italy in 1944, Army infantryman Johnson single-handedly held off five German paratroop companies. He killed 20 enemy soldiers, captured 25 others and rescued two fellow soldiers. Johnson died in 1998. *LSJ Archives*

▲ **Chavez in Lansing:** Civil rights activist Cesar Chavez was considered a friend by many Hispanics in the Lansing area. The United Farm Workers president spoke to an audience in Lansing, 1985. Lansing continues to celebrate Chavez' accomplishments with an annual Cesar Chavez dinner. *LSJ Archives*

◀ **A legacy is born:** The Rev. Dr. Martin Luther King Jr. addressed an MSU audience in March 1966. King's life and work are celebrated annually in Lansing. In the 1990s, the former Logan Street was renamed in King's honor. *Courtesy Norris Ingells*

▶ **Already famous:** By the time he graduated from the Michigan School for the Blind in 1968, pop singer Stevie Wonder was already a star. He lived in Lansing for several years while attending the school. *Courtesy Bruce Cornelius*

THE STATE JOURNAL

HOME EDITION
U.S. Weather Report
Cold, Low tonight 17. High Saturday 32.

Served by: Associated Press, United Press International, The New York Times and Los Angeles Times · Washington Post News Services

ONE HUNDRED-THIRTEENTH YEAR · LANSING—EAST LANSING, MICHIGAN, FRIDAY, APRIL 5, 1968 · 52 Pages · PRICE—TEN CENTS

Stunned U.S. Mourns King

Assassin Triggered Violence
By BRIAN SULLIVAN
Associated Press Writer

Dr. King When He Spoke at MSU in 1966

LBJ Plea Spurs Hunt For Slayer of Leader
By BILL JOHNSON

Changed History by Spirit
In Select Circle
By LOUIS CASSELS

President Summons Civil Rights Chiefs
WASHINGTON (AP)—President Johnson called on the nation today...

Bulletin
WASHINGTON (UPI)—President Johnson today proclaimed Sunday a national day of mourning for Dr. Martin Luther King Jr.

May 9 School Levy Set at Four Mills
By MARCIA VAN NESS
State Journal Education Writer

Lansing Planning Memorial Tributes

Khe Sanh No Longer Under Siege: Officer
SAIGON (AP)—The siege of Khe Sanh has been lifted...

Youth Exhibit Near End

Jury Finds Aikens Guilty of Murder
State Journal Eaton Bureau
CHARLOTTE—Gerald Alfred Aikens, 32, of Lansing, was found guilty of first degree murder by a jury in Eaton County Circuit Court, Thursday.

Freezing 17 Forecast For Area

'National Tragedy' —Romney

Inside The State Journal

Ann Landers B-4
Around-The-World A-2
Bridge Column A-6
Classified .... D-16 to D-17
Crossword Puzzle A-6
Editorials A-8, A-9
Family Living ...... B-1 to B-7
Home Journal D-1
Lansing Area A-16, A-17
People On The Move A-4
Sports D-4
Theater D-3
TV Listings A-3
Weather A-2

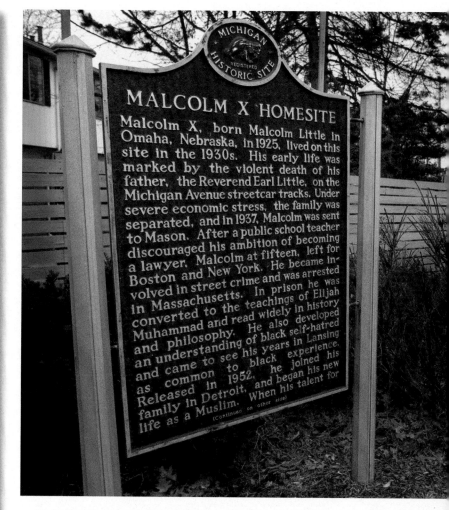

▲ **Malcolm X's home:** As a child, militant black leader Malcolm X (born Malcolm Little) lived in Lansing. His father was killed in a streetcar accident in Lansing. His famous "Autobiography of Malcolm X" reflected the family's life, and loss, while in Lansing and Mason. *LSJ Archives*

◄ **Slain:** The 1968 assassination of Martin Luther King Jr. sparked riots and violence in many cities. Lansing remained remarkably calm despite deep grief and anger over King's death in Memphis. *LSJ Archives*

▶ **Lansing native, Hollywood star:** Burt Reynolds turned up at an MSU football game in 1987, and chatted with coach George Perles (right) and Florida State coach Bobby Bowden. Reynolds lived in Lansing as a boy. *LSJ Archives*

◀ **Charter story:** Youngsters at New City Academy listen as a teacher reads a book in this 2004 photo. Charter schools were created by state law in the mid-1990s, part of statewide reforms that revamped how public schools were funded. *LSJ Archives*

▼ **End of an era:** BoarsHead Theatre co-founder John Peakes stars with veteran actor Carmen Decker in a 1984 production of "Time Steps." Peakes retired in 2004 after 36 years. Decker still performs with BoarsHead. *LSJ Archives*

▲ **Growing a college:** In 2000, Paula Cunningham became the first woman president of Lansing Community College. LCC is the third largest community college in Michigan. More than 19,000 full-time and part-time students attend LCC each semester. *LSJ Archives*

◀ **Top of their game:** Gov. Jennifer Granholm and MSU Provost Lou Anna Simon share a laugh before a convocation ceremony in 2003. Granholm is Michigan's first female governor. Simon was appointed MSU's first female president in 2004. She assumes the post on Jan. 1, 2005. *LSJ Archives*

▶ **Michigan legend:** Former Michigan Supreme Court Justice John Voelker was more famous for a novel written under the pen name Robert Traver, "Anatomy of a Murder." Voelker was the consummate trout fisherman who wrote about fishing travails and triumphs in his beloved Upper Peninsula. This photo was taken when Voelker visited Lansing in 1982. *Courtesy Norris Ingells*

▲ **'Lost' and found:** Sudanese orphans Clement Garang (left) and Peter Deng speak about their experiences in the American Midwest in 2000. They were among more than 120 "Lost Boys" who settled in the Lansing area. The humanitarian crisis in Sudan became the focus of international concern in 2004. Hundreds of thousands of Sudanese are thought to be targeted for genocide. *LSJ Archives*

◀ **A 'Cadillac' town:** Once known as an Oldsmobile town, Lansing now makes Cadillacs. Lansing Mayor Tony Benavides used GM's Grand River Assembly Plant as the back-drop for his 2004 State of the City address. Benavides is Lansing's first Hispanic mayor.

LSJ Archives

◀ ▲ **Google this:** On the road to becoming a billionaire, Google co-founder Larry Page is shown (left) as an East Lansing youngster, making widgets with LEGOs. In 2004 Google, the Internet's largest search engine, estimated the company's worth to be about $36 billion. *LSJ Archives*

CHAPTER SIX

Our Communities

A community may define itself in all sorts of ways: by the quality of its schools, its churches and civic organizations, the vibrancy of its business district.

What is intriguing about mid-Michigan communities is how many define themselves through celebrations.

No less than 40 festivals and fairs are scattered across the calendar. They've become annual traditions; long-standing traditions at that. The Ingham County Fair, for instance, celebrated its 150th anniversary in 2004.

Of course, there's more to a community than picnics and parades. Volunteering is big. You'll see folks painting houses for Habitat for Humanity, doing walk-a-thons for cancer research, picking up trash for Adopt A Highway and Adopt A River.

Pride percolates through communities, whether it's a fund-raiser to build a new playground or pride of heritage among those savoring their ethnic roots.

Even something as seemingly trivial as rescuing baby ducks from a sewer drain says something about the quality of a community's heart.

The photographs in this chapter reveal not just how mid-Michigan communities looked over these many years, but also how communities saw themselves. If there is a word to sum up those communal emotions, it's "hopeful."

◀ **Bricks were big:** This 1913 photograph reputedly shows Lansing's first Labor Day parade. Congress declared Labor Day a federal holiday in 1894. As the photo suggests, brick hauling was a lively trade in the early 20th century. *LSJ Archives*

▶ **Soaring spire:** Lansing's Plymouth Congregational Church in 1879. Fire destroyed the church in 1971. *Courtesy Capital Area District Library*

▲ **Prepped for parade:** Business entries for a Lansing parade in the late 19th century. *Courtesy MSU Museum History Division, 2924.1*

▶ **First Baptist Church:** One sign of a thriving community is when churches begin to appear. The First Baptist Church of Lansing, at the corner of Washington Avenue and Ionia Street, was dedicated in 1859 and remained in service until a new church was built in 1894. Photo, circa 1860. *Courtesy Capital Area District Library*

▲ **Universalist worship:** Downtown Lansing's First Universalist Church, once located at the corner of Grand Avenue and Allegan Street. The date of this photo is unknown. The church was dedicated in 1863. *Courtesy Capital Area District Library*

◀ **Union School:** This two-story schoolhouse was located at the corner of Townsend and Washtenaw streets. The photo was taken in 1879. *Courtesy Capital Area District Library*

Barnes home: An early resident of Lansing, O.I. Barnes, lived in this stately home, circa late 1800s. *Courtesy MSU Museum History Division, 70183.6.3*

▲ **Police arrive:** Though Lansing was established as a community by the 1850s, apparently it took some time for townsfolk to decide they needed a police department. Lansing's police department was first organized in 1893. The photo shows the entire police force. The boy on the tricycle, Claude Harrington, is the son of patrolman Ben Harrington, second from the right. *Courtesy Capital Area District Library*

◀ **School or mansion?** It's a school. Lansing High School, to be exact, circa late 1870s. The unique architecture appears to blend Victorian and French influences. *Courtesy MSU Museum History Division, 7018.6.1*

▲ **Railroads' golden age:** Trains were the lifeblood of far-flung communities. They were a common sight in Lansing, as seen in this photo, circa 1870, taken in North Lansing. Note the youngster sitting on the locomotive's "cow catcher." *LSJ Archives*

◀ **First Pilgrim Congregational Church:** At one time located at the corner of Michigan Avenue and Larch Street, the church originally had been the Larch Street School. Services began in the church in 1893. *Courtesy Capital Area District Library*

▶ **Civil War remembrance:** Union Army veterans marched in a parade in Lansing, circa 1910, about 50 years after the bloody War Between the States began. *LSJ Archives*

▲ **Pioneers remembered:** A tiny log cabin atop a wagon seems a fitting tribute to the pioneer past, part of a 1913 Pioneer Day in Lansing. The man standing with a rifle his father made is identified as J.N. Bush. *Courtesy Capital Area District Library*

▲ **Now boarding:** Passengers prepare to depart on the Waverly Park Steamer in 1905. The excursion boat plied the Grand River, and docked near what is now Waverly Road and Moores River Drive. *Courtesy Capital Area District Library*

▼ **One-room schoolhouse:** Country schools were ubiquitous well into the 20th century. This is the entire student body of Pink School in 1919. The school was located at the corner of Columbia and College roads. *Courtesy Jim Munro collection*

▲ **Ox-powered:** Even as the Automobile Age approached, some mid-Michigan residents relied on ox-drawn wagons for transportation. This photo was taken in the late 1800s. *LSJ Archives*

▲ **'Infamy' recalled:** On Dec. 7, 1991 – 50 years after Japan attacked Pearl Harbor – veterans gathered in the Lansing area to remember the "day of infamy." Here, Bob Evans of VFW Post 4005 plays "Taps." *LSJ Archives*

◄ **Extra!** Stunned readers learned the details of an attack that would change their lives. *LSJ Archives*

▼ **On patrol:** One of Ingham County's first patrol cars stops in at the Lansing Drive-in movie theater on South Cedar Street in 1949. Behind the wheel is Deputy Robert Lorencen. Standing alongside is Deputy Alvin Hartig. *Courtesy Jim Monro collection*

▲ **On the march:** A Grand Ledge band marches past during Lansing's centennial parade in 1959. *LSJ Archives*

▲ **Holiday charity:** The Crippled Children Committee holds its Christmas party at the Hotel Olds on Dec. 21, 1945. From left: Clarence Neitz, Hugo Lundberg, Christian Herrmann, Herman Lucas, Charles Burlingham, Alpheus Maxson and Christian Roosenraad. An eighth person is unidentified. *Courtesy Jim Munro collection*

◄ **Don't be fooled:** What appears to be a scene gleaned from a 19th-century farm field is actually a re-enactment. During MSU's centennial in 1955, actors portrayed harvesting techniques of the mid-19th century. Look closely: A more modern harvesting machine is in the background. *Courtesy MSU Museum History Division*

▸ **Construction zone:** Lansing underwent a massive disruption during the construction of Interstate 496 in the late 1960s. Several historic homes were demolished in the process. This 1969 aerial view is of the I-496/Creyts Road intersection west of Lansing. *LSJ Archives*

▶ **Tiny parade-goer:** Two-year-old Elizabeth Gao of East Lansing gets a comfy seat to watch Lansing's 1994 Fourth of July Parade. Providing the seat is her father, Longying Gao. *LSJ Archives*

▲ ▶ **Michigan Festival:** Before there was a Common Ground festival, or a Great Lakes Folk Festival, there was the Michigan Festival. From 1987 to 1997, the weeklong mix of music concerts and folk art drew tens of thousands of people to MSU's campus each day. Above: The crowd awaits a head-liner act at the 1987 Michigan Festival. Right: Amish furniture maker Roy Yoder and son Merle, of Elsie, demonstrate how to bend a hickory stick for a rock-ing chair. You couldn't beat Michigan Festival's price: Some years, $10 got you in for the whole week. Low ticket prices proved to be the festival's undoing. It declared bankruptcy in 1998. *LSJ Archives*

◀ **Majestic courthouse:** Mid-Michigan is home to several historic courthouses. The Eaton County Courthouse in Charlotte was built in 1885. Shown here in a 1954 photo, it was later acquired by the Courthouse Square Association when new county offices were built in 1976. *LSJ Archives*

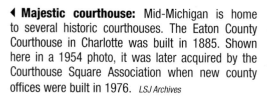

Play ball! Oldsmobile Park, home of the Lansing Lugnuts, opened in 1996. The city-financed, $12.7-million stadium brings thousands of people to the downtown area each spring and summer to watch the minor league baseball team. Above: A crowd lines up outside the park to buy advance tickets for opening day. Below: Private donations paid for the bronze statue, "Hometown Hero," which graces the lawn in front of Oldsmobile Park. *LSJ Archives*

River revival: Linda Morgano of Okemos and John Slack of Mt. Pleasant volunteer their morning to remove trash from the Grand River during Adopt A River Day in 1996. Left: Ricardo Briones removes a junked TV found along Lansing's River Trail in this 1997 photo. Each spring and fall, hundreds of volunteers turn out for Adopt A River Day, to clean and beautify the Grand and Red Cedar rivers. Adopt A River began in 1994 following a series of Lansing State Journal editorials suggesting a program similar to Michigan's Adopt A Highway program.

LSJ Archives

91

◀ ▲ Michigan hot and cold: A frosty veneer coats the trees near the MSU horse barns in 1999. Left: In warmer days, youngsters take advantage of fountain sprays at Moores Park Pool in July 1997. *LSJ Archives*

▶ Animal house: Hard to believe, but this 129-year-old house in north Lansing was once the winter quarters for a local circus. Lions, zebras and elephants inhabited the grounds. The circus was owned by a former Lansing mayor, Joseph Warner. Warner is reputed to have discovered Jumbo, billed by Barnum & Bailey Circus as the world's largest elephant. Shown here in 2004: Current owner Robert LaMacchia. He's renovating the Warner House, one of Lansing's oldest.

LSJ Archives

▲ **Lion down:** Children check out Potter Park Zoo's lion as he dozes atop his rocky domain. *LSJ Archives*

▼ **Toe-tappin' time:** After a three-year run of hosting the National Folk Festival, MSU and East Lansing decided to further the tradition by creating the Great Lakes Folk Festival. The August event brings national and international artists to the streets of East Lansing, as well as a number of Michigan artists and craftsmen. Here, fiddler Lucy MacNeil kicks off the 2003 festival on a Friday evening. *LSJ Archives*

▲ **Llama-rama:** A youngster gets into a stare-down contest with a llama at Lansing's Potter Park Zoo. The zoo is one of mid-Michigan's top attractions, with more than 360,000 visitors each year. *LSJ Archives*

▲ **Duck down:** Six ducklings swept into a sewer drain brought rescuers to the scene in downtown Lansing in July 2000. Police cadet Aaron Terrill went head-first into the drain while Lansing Area Search and Rescue's Leroy Nestell held on. Five of the six ducklings were reunited with their mother, who was pacing (and waddling) close by. *LSJ Archives*

▶ **Cinco de Mayo:** The Mexican holiday has been transported to the Lansing area, which has a thriving Hispanic population. Here, El Grupo Fiesta dancers perform at Lansing Community College in 2001. *LSJ Archives*

▲ **Roughing it (or pretending to):** Boy Scouts Cody Huffman (left) and Sean Hammond settle in for a spell at the campfire during the 2003 scouting Winter Jamboree near Mason. *LSJ Archives*

◀ **Common Ground:** 2000 began a new millennium, and a new festival for Lansing. Common Ground features a week of music and other events each July at Riverfront Park. Thousands turn out for nightly concerts; here, ZZ Top cranks out a tune in 2004. *LSJ Archives*

◀ **Chili forecast:** Rain or shine, the annual Chili Cook Off along Lansing's riverfront delivers heat to eager taste buds. The one-evening event in June pits restaurants vying for best chili awards. Proceeds go to local charities. *LSJ Archives*

▶ **An end and a beginning:** A warm hug welcomes newly minted graduate Erin McCue in 2004. The Lansing Sexton High School grad is embraced by math teacher Sue Herner, who just retired after teaching at Sexton since 1981. *LSJ Archives*

▲ **Star-spangled:** Kendra Lilly's hair is awash with patriotism as she watches the 2004 Memorial Day parade in Dansville. *LSJ Archives*

▶ **Soap story:** The last day of school for Grand Ledge High School seniors means it's time for – what else? – a shaving cream fight. It's a spring rite for seniors. Here, Katie Bell (left) and Meghan Egan show off their new do's in 2004.

LSJ Archives

◀ **Chopping spree:** Youngsters take a whack at learning Michigan's pioneer past at the 2003 American Heritage Festival at the Woldumar Nature Center. *LSJ Archives*

▲ **Memorial Day:** 1993 marked the 125th anniversary of the first Memorial Day. Here, the Department of Michigan Sons of Union Veterans of the Civil War Color Guard march to the steps of the Capitol. *LSJ Archives*

CHAPTER SEVEN

Disaster

A mad bomber. A blizzard followed by torrential rains. A hotel fire racing to the uppers floors toward unsuspecting guests.

Such were the seeds of local tragedy, heartache and loss.

Lansing and its surrounding communities have suffered their share of disasters, both man-made and by nature's hand. In terms of sheer horror, no local disaster rivals the events of one May morning in 1927. Some 500 pounds of dynamite, secretly planted inside the Bath schoolhouse, were ignited. Forty-five people were killed, most of them schoolchildren just days away from summer vacation. The bomber, a disgruntled school board member, later killed himself.

In terms of impact on the entire community, Lansing's floods have no equal. The worst of them to hit this river city were in 1904, 1947 and 1975. The April 1975 flood started with a 13-inch snowfall, followed soon after by 5 inches of rain. The ground was saturated. The water above ground gushed into the Grand and Red Cedar rivers, which inexorably overflowed their banks.

The Greater Lansing community was declared a federal disaster area. More than 600 families needed varying degrees of help. Losses to homes and businesses exceeded $48 million.

It's a cliché – but nonetheless true – that disasters often bring out the best in a community. That certainly was the case in the 1975 flood. Hundreds of volunteers and thousands of dollars in donations helped victims pick up the pieces.

Charity cannot blot out a disaster's painful memories. It can, however, help the human spirit endure.

◀ ▶ **School bombed:** On May 18, 1927, a horrific blast tore through the Bath schoolhouse (left). Disgruntled school board member Andrew Kehoe ignited 500 pounds of dynamite he had planted inside the school. The bombing killed 45 people – 38 of them schoolchildren. Kehoe killed himself later that day. Until the Oklahoma City bombing in 1995, the Bath school disaster was the deadliest act of terrorism in U.S. history. Right: A shocked and grief-stricken community begins the process of identifying the victims. *LSJ Archives*

High water marks: One of Lansing's worst floods occurred in March 1904. Above: Floodwaters felled the Kalamazoo Street bridge, which was swept downstream and under the Michigan Avenue Bridge. Below: A flooded Lansing street. *LSJ Archives*

Archives lost: Fire swept through the State of Michigan Library in February 1951, destroying or virtually ruining countless books and other documents. Opposite page: Parts of the library collection were taken to a nearby gymnasium, where salvaging efforts began. Still, the state lost priceless records of the past. *Courtesy Jim Munro Collection (above), LSJ Archives (right)*

◀ Tragic fire: A blaze raced through Lansing's Kerns Hotel on Dec. 11, 1934, trapping dozens of people on the upper floors. Authorities were never certain how many people perished. Thirty-four bodies were recovered, making it the deadliest fire in the city's history. At first, a carelessly tossed cigarette was blamed, but officials later backed away from that conclusion. The hotel was located at the corner of Grand Avenue and Ottawa Street. *LSJ Archives*

▶ Tornado strikes: An unidentified woman holds her child on the steps of what was once their home. The April 1967 tornado cut a violent swath across the St. Johns area. *LSJ Archives*

◀ Record snow: On Jan. 26, 1967, a blizzard clobbered Lansing with 20.4 inches on the ground — a record. It would be several days before residential streets such as this one were plowed. *LSJ Archives*

▶ 'Ghost town': That's how the front page of the State Journal described Midwestern communities such as Lansing, which was buried in the city's worst-ever blizzard on Jan. 26, 1967. The mayor declared a state of emergency, and life did not return to normal for several days. *LSJ Archives*

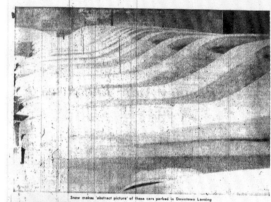

THE STATE JOURNAL

HOME EDITION
U.S. Weather Report.

Served by Associated Press, United Press International, The New York Times and Los Angeles Times - Washington Post News Services

ONE HUNDRED - TWELFTH YEAR   LANSING—EAST LANSING, MICHIGAN, FRIDAY, JANUARY 27, 1967   8 PAGES   PRICE—TEN CENTS

State of Emergency Declared In Lansing's Worst Blizzard

Snowdrifts Shut Factories, Stores

By CURT HANES and JIM HOUGH
State Journal Staff Writers

The most paralyzing snowfall in Lansing history shocked and exhausted residents this morning, and not much relief is expected before Saturday.

Nearly 24 inches of snow were on the ground by noon here and the U.S. Weather Bureau said from two to four more inches will fall before tonight.

Mayor Murninghan declared a state of emergency in Lansing this morning.

He urged all residents to stay in their homes or work in their neighborhoods to shovel out fire hydrants and move stalled cars from the streets. He asked all businessmen to close their businesses today, except those whose services were considered vital.

The area's most ghastly storm since 1921 was blamed on the death of at least two persons, brought on a super-human effort by public servants and private persons and a paralysis which may not end for days.

City plow crews fought a losing battle all night as the storm created blizzard conditions with wind gusts up to 40 miles per hour. Drifts up to 10 feet high were reported by mid-morning.

Dozens of emergencies, building cave-ins, personal heroics, and thousands of personal experiences will mark this generation as the one which witnessed the 'Blizzard of '67.'

Manufacturing plants and businesses were generally closed today. Oldsmobile employes were asked as early as Thursday evening to stay home. Fisher Body plant employes also were asked to stay home.

In addition, most other plants and offices in the area were closed today.

Few, if any, state offices were operating today, although they were not closed by any official proclamation, according to State Police.

Snow makes 'abstract picture' of these cars parked in Downtown Lansing

Midwest Looks Like Huge Ghost Town

By The Associated Press

Walking is the surest way

Firemen To Check Buildings

Fire Chief Victor Space said the Fire Prevention Bureau would be out Friday afternoon checking buildings for snow accumulation and evidence of stress, particularly the big shopping complexes.

Space also said the department was receiving many calls from persons who said they got furnaces were coming on with a whirring noise.

The chief said these furnaces were suffocating for lack of makeup air and he suggested residents clear the snow from the basement window and open it to let air in so the furnace can breathe.

Personnel, Equipment

National Guard Aiding in Storm

FIREMEN KEPT BUSY

Fire Chief Victor Space sought to meet the emergency conditions by placing firemen on double shifts. He said any serious fire had been reported by mid-morning today, but his men were kept busy with ambulance calls and assists at businesses where roofs caved in from heavy snow pressure.

Lansing Snow Sets Record

Howard Chrisinat, who worked a double shift at the U.S. Weather Bureau, reported 21 inches of snow on the ground here at 1 p.m. today.

A few miles away in the twin cities of Champaign-Urbana, the University of Illinois education station hour at 300-foot tower.

Other heavy 24-hour snowfalls here were 11 inches in Nov., 1951; 11 inches in March, 1946; 12 inches in March, 1951; 13 inches in May, 1932; 13 in March, 1919; 11 in Jan., 1916; and 12 in Feb., 1912.

Seek Rescue Of 27 on Bus

By LLOYD J. MOLES
State Journal Staff Writer

State Police, National Guardsmen and Delta Township firemen today were attempting to rescue 27 passengers stranded on a Greyhound bus at the Saginaw Highway and I-96 interchange since 12 p.m. Thursday.

Officers said they would attempt to take the people off the bus probably one-by-one on snowmobile and remove them to the Delta Fire Station about a quarter of a mile away.

The driver reported that the fuel was starting to run low and when depleted would leave them with no heat in the bus.

TELL PLIGHT OF BUS

Blizzard causes many a traffic jam, especially during the evening rush hours

▲ **Fiery show:** One of Lansing's more spectacular fires lit up an early morning sky on August 29, 1977. The northside blaze at Lansing Ice and Fuel sent flames about 400 feet into the air. No one was injured. Fire officials had to draw water from the nearby Grand River – an indication of the fire's size and ferocity. *LSJ Archives*

▶ **Up in smoke:** An entire block of downtown Ovid was consumed by a fire in 1990. *LSJ Archives*

▼ ▶ **The flood of '75:** In April 1975, heavy snow followed closely by torrential rain caused the Grand and Red Cedar rivers to overflow their banks. Parts of Lansing and Meridian Township were flooded, damaging scores of homes. Below: A Lansing resident surveys his neighborhood, under several feet of water. Right: An eastside Lansing street corner under more than 6 feet of water. *Courtesy Norris Ingells*

THE STATE JOURNAL
MICHIGAN'S COMPLETE NEWSPAPER
SUNDAY, APRIL 20, 1975, LANSING, MICHIGAN   PRICE—40 CENTS

Worst Flood Since 1947 Hits

Raging Grand was up to Mrs. Sally Wainman's River Street door Saturday afternoon

Flood of '75 Real to Those Along Rivers

Justice Thomas Kavanagh Dies

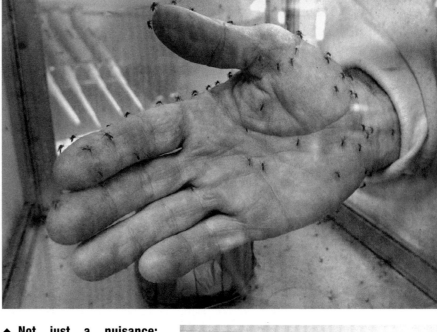

▲ Not just a nuisance: Mosquitoes are regarded as more than pests these days. The biting insects are sometimes infected with the West Nile virus. In Michigan in 2003, 19 people contracted the virus; two died. That was far below 2002, when Michigan had 644 cases and 51 deaths linked to West Nile. *LSJ Archives*

◄ City under water: The flood and its aftermath consumed LSJ coverage for several weeks. The State Journal and WJIM-TV Channel 6 co-sponsored a telethon that raised thousands of dollars to assist flood victims. *LSJ Archives*

► Off the track: In one of the Lansing area's worst train derailments, 16 cars from a Grand Truck Western freight train jumped the tracks near Haslett in July 1988. *LSJ Archives*

▲ Dry times: Periodic droughts parch lawns and farm fields across mid-Michigan. In 2001, lack of rain stunted the growth of ears of field corn, taking a bite out of crop yields.

LSJ Archives

▶ Fateful day: It was one of those chilling scenes of horror that no living American will forget. The 9/11 terrorist attacks on the World Trade Center and the Pentagon would forever alter American attitudes and government policy.

LSJ Archives

INSIDE: Complete coverage in special 8-page section

Lansing State Journal
* Wednesday
September 12, 2001
www.lsj.com
50¢

U.S. UNDER ATTACK

DAY OF TERROR HORRIFIES U.S.

Time line

9:03 a.m.

World Trade Center
An aircraft is seen moments before it crashes into the World Trade Center. It appeared just minutes after another crashed into one of the twin towers.

9:40 a.m.

The Pentagon
Smoke and flames rise over the Pentagon in Washington, D.C., following the crash of a commercial airliner into a heliport near the building.

9:50 a.m.

World Trade Center
The south tower of the World Trade Center collapses, sending debris flying and people scurrying through the streets to find safety.

10 a.m.

Shanksville, Pa.
A United Airlines aircraft is hijacked after leaving Newark, N.J., and crashes in Pennsylvania, killing all 45 people aboard.

Stunning blow: Smoke billows from one of the towers of the World Trade Center as flames and debris explode from the second tower Tuesday in New York. In the most devastating attack ever against the United States, terrorists crashed two planes into the twin towers in a pair of deadly blows that brought down the 110-story towers.

CHAO SOI CHEONG/Associated Press

Inside

Onslaught shakes U.S. to its core
Worst terrorist attack in American history leaves thousands suspected dead.
Page 5A

Religious groups gather to grieve
Mid-Michigan faith communities offer their prayers and condolences.
Page 6A

World reacts to U.S. tragedy
Most nations offer condolences while others cheer attacks on U.S. landmarks.
Page 10A

Attacks heighten state security
State closes buildings to visitors after attacks in New York and Washington, D.C.
Page 11A

Inside
Local **B**   Sports **C**
Living **D**   Classified **S**
Ann Landers 2D
Business 5C
Movie ads 2D
Opinion 14A

CHAPTER EIGHT

Changing Times

Americans are fascinated by change.

Sometimes it's a better mousetrap – "the next new thing." At other times, we are a rapt audience, or passionate participants, in historic change.

More than once, Lansing has been swept up in these societal crosscurrents. The abolition of slavery. Women's suffrage. The rise of labor unions. Prohibition. The Great Depression. Civil rights. Anti-war protests.

Michigan's capital city is always ripe for the "perfect storm" of politics and public spectacle. Here, the seat of Michigan government. A few miles east of here: a major university, cauldron of provocative ideas. The Capitol becomes the logical nexus for all sorts of public demonstrations.

One of the first massive demonstrations in Lansing history took place during the famous Labor Holiday of 1937. Some 20,000 workers virtually shut down the city in protest of the arrest of union pickets.

Fresher in living memory are the anti-war protests of 1969 and 1970, when thousands of demonstrators marched from Michigan State University down Michigan Avenue to the Capitol.

Not all of the protests were peaceful. In 1989, protesters blocking an entrance to a Lansing abortion clinic were arrested. And a 1994 Ku Klux Klan rally at the Capitol drew hundreds of anti-Klan demonstrators. Rocks were thrown, eight demonstrators were arrested, and police used pepper spray to thwart protesters.

Democracy is not always tidy. Nonetheless, at the heart of all this confrontation IS democracy; a free people exercising their right to be heard on the streets of Michigan's capital.

◀ **Running for president:** Bobby Kennedy was making a strong bid for the White House when he flew in for a Lansing rally in April 1968. At his side: then-Lansing Councilman Joel Ferguson, now an MSU trustee. Less than two months later, Kennedy was assassinated. *Courtesy Bruce Cornelius*

▶ **Abortion protest:** An anti-abortion activist is arrested by Lansing police in July 1989. Protesters were blocking the entrance to Womancare, where abortions were performed. *LSJ Archives*

THE STATE JOURNAL

Sixteen Pages
144 Columns

EIGHTY-THIRD YEAR • • • LANSING, MICHIGAN, MONDAY, JUNE 7, 1937 PRICE—THREE CENTS

The Weather:
Partly cloudy and cooler tonight and Tuesday; fair and continued cool Wednesday.

HOLIDAY CLOSES CITY

ADVANCE GUARD OF TEMPLARS IN CITY FOR MEET

'Labor Holiday' Unlikely to Interfere with Conclave, State Leaders Believe

VARIED PROGRAM OPENS

Union Promises Aid to Templars

City's Main Corners Blocked as 'Holiday' Starts

Governor Seeking Settlement Of Issues Behind UAW Tie-Up Caused By Arrest of Pickets

UAW Explains 'Labor Holiday'

Murphy Seeks 'Facts' Relative to Jailing of Eight Unionists by Deputies; Local Plants, Business Places Generally Closed in Huge Demonstration

OIL EXPLOSION TWO ARE KILLED KILLS WOMAN IN PLANE CRASH

Fowlerville Resident Dies In Local Hospital as Result of Burns

Tragic Accident Blamed on Overloading, Small Ship Nose Dives, Burns

'Holiday Protest At Injustice' — Homer Martin

Headline said it all: On June 7, 1937, some 20,000 Lansing workers demonstrated in a citywide Labor Holiday. The virtual strike shut down the city and made national news. The rally/strike was precipitated by the arrest of union pickets and their wives. The commotion was so great that the state Senate, meeting nearby in the Capitol, decided to adjourn. *LSJ Archives*

War, on the home front: In World War II, men fought the war with guns and the women fought it with industrial production. "Rosie the Riveter" was the generic name given to the strong, competent women who made U.S. military might second to none. For the poster rendition of Rosie, the artist used a photo of Lansing resident Geraldine Doyle, whose contributions were honored by the Michigan Senate in 2002. *LSJ Archives*

▲ **Black and white:** A 1963 NCAA regional basketball game at MSU had political overtones. The governor of Mississippi objected to Mississippi State's white team playing Loyola (Ill.), some of whose players were black. The Mississippi State team sneaked out of the state in order to play in the tournament. It was considered the first interracial collegiate basketball game. Loyola won – and went on to win the NCAA championship.

Courtesy Norris Ingells

◀ ▶ **Protests of a different kind:** There's more to protests than anti-war demonstrations. Left: Farmers rallied at the Capitol in 1985 to bring attention to the plight of farmers and farming communities. Right: Bikers in 1988 burned helmets to protest a law that requires motorcyclists to wear helmets. The "Let those who ride decide" movement has held annual protests at the Capitol. *LSJ Archives*

**▲ Defiance personi-
fied:** With a rebellious
glare, an unidentified
protester takes a puff
near the steps of the
state Capitol. Thousands
joined in the protest on
May 14, 1970, 10 days
after four students were
killed at Kent State.

Courtesy Bruce Cornelius

▶ Art imitates life:
Street theater mir-
rors President Nixon's
famous victory gesture
in this protest by the
Streetcorner Society. The
protest-theater troupe
staged political satire
on the MSU campus in
1970. *Courtesy Bruce Cornelius*

▲ Running for president – again: Richard Nixon campaigned for election in June 1968 at the
Lansing Civic Center, having lost in 1960 to John F. Kennedy. Nixon won this time, narrowly defeating
Vice President Hubert Humphrey. *Courtesy Bruce Cornelius*

Anti-porn: Protesters including Lansing Mayor Terry McKane marched in August 1984 against Lansing's "sin strip." Eventually, the porn merchants relocated away from Michigan Avenue. Today, the sin strip is pretty tame; restaurants, Oldsmobile Park and the Lansing Center occupy places where adult bookstores once stood. *LSJ Archives*

Police, strikers clash: Early on the morning of Feb. 11, 1974, striking Motor Wheel workers attempted to block nonstriking employees from entering the plant. Helmeted Lansing police, equipped with riot gear, waded into the crowd of strikers. A bloody clash ensued, and two pickets were sent to the hospital. The melee contributed to a bitter two-month strike. Motor Wheel once employed 3,500 people. When it shuttered its Lansing plant in 1996, fewer than 200 workers remained. *LSJ Archives*

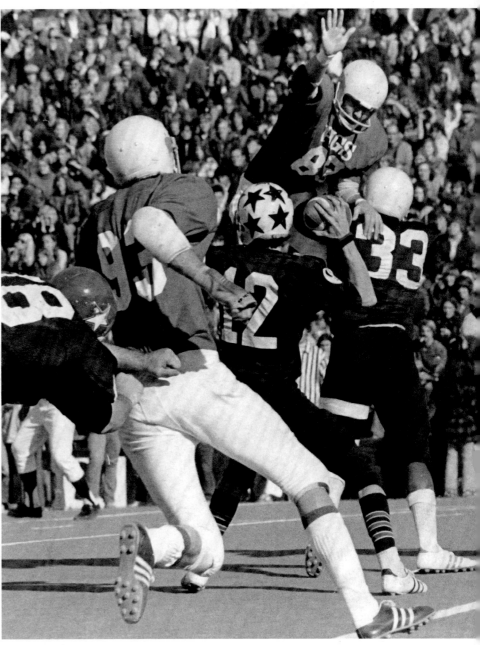

Tension release: What began as a way to ease tensions between East Lansing police and hippies became an annual football charity game. The first game between the "pigs" and "freaks" was in the early 1970s. This photo was taken in 1973. *LSJ Archives*

CHAPTER NINE

Serious Fun

How people relax and play says nearly as much about a community as how it works.

Look around mid-Michigan, and you soon know this populace is serious about its fun.

More than 60 golf courses are scattered across six counties, any one of which is within a 45-minute drive of Lansing. In the cooler seasons, bowling alleys are packed with league action. In summers, scores of softball fields are alive with leagues for youngsters and those still young at heart. There are soccer leagues, a sailing club and hunting clubs; euchre tournaments, pool tournaments and bingo nights.

On many summer weekends, you can run a 5K race in the morning, attend a car meet in the afternoon, and leave time for a nap before catching an evening game of baseball at Oldsmobile Park.

And speaking of parks ... we have skate parks, a dog park, nature parks, a state park, swim parks, scores of city, county and township parks ... and a "linear park" called the River Trail. It's one of the nation's longest urban river trails.

Plus runners, bikers and walkers *everywhere*.

At the top of many people's sports list are the MSU Spartans, with all the attendant excitement Spartan teams bring to the court, field and rink.

Many of us remember where we were when Magic Johnson led MSU to the 1979 NCAA title. Yet, how many remember when MSU had a polo team? Some sports and leisure traditions are intact. Others have long faded. The following pages catch glimpses of both.

◀ **There was a time ...** when polo was popular on the Michigan State campus. Shown here: the first MSU polo team, 1929. *Courtesy MSU Museum History Division, 1996:183.10.1*

▶ **The old ballgame:** If you had a college, it seems, you had to have a baseball team. That certainly was true in the early decades of the 20th century. This is Michigan Agricultural College's team, circa 1915. *Courtesy MSU Museum History Division, Blake Miller Family*

THE STATE JOURNAL
SUNDAY EDITION

WEATHER
Partly sunny, warmer. High 44, low 25-30.

ONE HUNDRED-TWELFTH YEAR ★ ★ ★   LANSING—EAST LANSING, MICHIGAN, SUNDAY, NOVEMBER 20, 1966   158 Pages

University parking lots were jammed Saturday with football fans' cars.

Huge 'Poll' Crowd Leaves Unsatisfied

By NORRIS INGELLS
State Journal Staff Writer

The Other Ones

Believe it or not, several other football games were played Saturday besides that at East Lansing.

UCLA 14, SOUTHERN CAL 7

MICHIGAN 17, OHIO STATE 3

PURDUE 51, INDIANA 6

WISCONSIN 7, MINNESOTA 6

NORTHWESTERN 35, ILLINOIS 7

CENTRAL MICHIGAN 44, WAYNE 0

Part of record crowd en route to stadium.

Shake-Up Hits S. Viet Forces

Ten Hunters Die In Deer 'Opening'

By Journal Wire Services

Romney Flies South To Meet GOP Heads

Freighter Grounded In Huron

Two Viets Removed From Jobs

U.N. Limits For Israel Called For

Labor's Voice Not Silenced

By JERRY MORAL
State Journal Capitol Bureau

Warmer, Sunny Skies Due Here

Treasures Hit by Flood

Group Rescuing Art

where to look

▲ **Easy, Jud:** Known for his vein-popping demeanor on the basketball court, MSU's Jud Heathcote was also known for getting results. Exhibit A: With Magic Johnson and Gregory Kelser in charge, the Spartans won the 1979 NCAA basketball championship. Heathcote's MSU career spanned 19 years, during which he compiled a 340-220 record. That makes him the winningest basketball coach in MSU history. *LSJ Archives*

◄ **Game of the century:** Or so it was called. The 1966 showdown at Spartan Stadium between MSU and Notre Dame was a clash of two undefeated teams. Both were ranked No. 1 at some point during the season. The game settled nothing. A crowd of more than 80,000 watched the two teams battle to a 10-10 tie. *LSJ Archives*

▶ **Duffy:** No other football coach in MSU history was as adored by fans as Duffy Daugherty. During 19 years as the Spartan head coach, he won four national championships. His 1965-66 teams were 19-1-1. Daugherty's wit was legendary. When a reporter asked at the beginning of a season whom he was happiest to see returning, Daugherty quickly replied: "Me." *LSJ Archives*

▲ ▶ **Ride's over:** The end of Lake Lansing's amusement park came with the thud of a wrecking crane in 1978. There were happier times. Kids went for a joyous ride on the roller coaster in 1973 (right). Part of the amusement park lives on, however. The beloved Lake Lansing carousel was sold to Cedar Point Amusement Park in Ohio, and was later moved to Dorney Park in Allentown, Pa. *LSJ Archives*

▲ ▶ ▶▶ **The one and only:** Lansing native Earvin "Magic" Johnson in February of his sophomore year at Michigan State University (above). Right: Magic soars for a layup during the 1979 season at MSU. The Spartans won their first NCAA championship that year. Opposite page: Fans mobbed Magic at Capital City Airport when the team returned from the title game. Magic was given his nickname by LSJ sportswriter Fred Stabley Jr. when Johnson was a junior at Lansing Everett High School. *LSJ Archives*

Rose Bowl victors: The last time MSU won a Rose Bowl? 1988. Above: MSU place-kicker John Langeloh (No. 10) celebrates his winning field goal over the University of Southern California, with punter Greg Montgomery at his side. Left: Spartan fans celebrate the victory. *LSJ Archives*

▶ **The River Trail in 1993:** Lansing's River Trail, seen here in 1993, follows the Grand and Red Cedar rivers between Lansing and East Lansing. About seven miles long, this urban river trail – one of the nation's longest – is popular with bikers, joggers and in-line skaters. *LSJ Archives*

▲ **Ice in their veins:** The Miller family of East Lansing has more than a love of hockey in their blood. They have the talent to match. Ten of the clan have played hockey at Michigan State; four of them went on to play in the National Hockey League. This familial hockey dynasty includes (from left) brothers Kevin, Kelly and Kip, photographed in 1987. *LSJ Archives*

▶ **Grand fun:** Canoe races were a highlight of Riverfest, an annual late-summer celebration along the Grand River during the 1980s. *LSJ Archives*

◀ **Tennis pro:** East Lansing native Todd Martin frequently returned from the pro circuit to conduct tennis clinics with area schoolchildren. In this 1996 photo, Martin breaks the ice with a shy Stephanie Stumpos, age 8. Martin retired from professional tennis in 2004. *LSJ Archives*

▶ **The guy can pitch:** Waverly High School pitcher John Smoltz celebrates winning the Diamond Classic championship in 1985. Smoltz has had a standout career in the major leagues: Cy Young Award winner, National League strikeout leader in 1992, and Most Valuable Player in the 1992 National League Championship Series. He pitched for the Atlanta Braves in several World Series games. *LSJ Archives*

▲ **Soccer soars:** Soccer's popularity has zoomed in Greater Lansing in the past decade. In this 2001 photo, Okemos' Jessica King (left) races for the ball with East Lansing's Carrie Fahey in a tournament for girls under age 12. *LSJ Archives*

◀ **Victory leap:** Dottie Pepper jumps for joy when her 60-foot birdie putt drops in, securing a victory in the 1999 Oldsmobile Classic. From 1992 to 2000, the LPGA tournament at East Lansing's Walnut Hills Country Club brought many of the world's best women golfers to mid-Michigan. *LSJ Archives*

For complete coverage
Full coverage of the Spartans' quest for a title in a four-page special section wrapped around Sports.

MICHIGAN STATE

Celebrate with the Spartans
Festivities begin at noon Wednesday at the Capitol, followed by a parade at 1 p.m. Page 2A

Tuesday
April 4, 2000
50¢

Lansing State Journal
www.lansingstatejournal.com

SPECIAL NCAA CHAMPIONSHIP FRONT PAGE

NATIONAL CHAMPS!

Savoring the moment: The 2000 NCAA Tournament champions Michigan State University Spartans beat the Gators 89-76 to capture the university's first national title since 1979. Thousands of fans celebrate after their win over Florida on Monday at the RCA Dome in Indianapolis. The Spartans flooded the streets of East Lansing after the game to celebrate the victory.

Spartans pound Gators 89-76 to win NCAA title

By Mark Mayes
Lansing State Journal

INDIANAPOLIS — As MSU players danced on the court, his Howard Stanley climbed atop his chair and reached his hand-painted sign toward the sky.

"Dreams can come true."

A gutty, determined Spartans team proved it Monday and throughout the NCAA Tournament. And the fans who witnessed Michigan State's run

to college basketball's national title could hardly believe they weren't still dreaming.

They hugged, howled and snapped pictures, trying to preserve a moment they wished could last forever.

"Some day we're going to be able to tell our kids how Mo Pete's dunks shook the arena!" screamed Gavin Matecki, 23, an MSU senior from Bear Lake.

This Spartan team — which steamrolled Florida, 89-76, for the title — will live on in legend.

For the way it responded to expectations that it should win the championship. For the way it stormed back after falling behind in early tournament games. For the way senior forward Morris Peterson showed his heart and his passion in the face of the loss of his grandmother during the tournament.

"You just don't know the emotion," said Peterson's mother, Valerie, as her daughter, Tonda, scrawled out a cardboard sign reading: "This one's

for your grandma."

The championship was MSU's first since 1979, when Lansing's Earvin "Magic" Johnson was the star.

Gov. John Engler promised a big celebration in Lansing after the team returns home today. Celebrations are planned at noon Wednesday at the Capitol and 2:30 p.m. Wednesday at Spartan Stadium.

"It's going to be a great victory party," Engler said. "This whole state is going to

celebrate."

Flint will join the celebration, holding a victory parade for its players: Peterson, Mateen Cleaves and Charlie Bell, said Cleaves' mother, Fran Cleaves, who followed her son to every game of his college career.

Kelly Rogers, 26, an MSU graduate student, proved prophetic when she tied a rope around the neck of a stuffed alligator and donned a sign calling herself the "Gator Strangler."

"It hasn't been since '79' that

MSU has played for the national championship, said Rogers. "so it's time to pull out the stops."

Ben Hartnell, 22, an MSU senior, waved a sign reading "Citrus Bowl Sequel" to signify how the Spartans have beaten Florida twice this year. The football team downed Florida 37-34 in the Jan. 1 Florida Citrus Bowl.

"It hasn't even sunk in yet," Hartnell said. "I'll wake up tomorrow and realize (a) we won the national championship, and (b) I was there."

Back to Lansing
The Spartans are expected to touch down at Capital City Airport at 2:48 p.m. today.

HOME DELIVERY: 1-800-234-1719

◀ ▲ **The victors:** MSU basketball coach Tom Izzo beams and Mateen Cleaves gets teary-eyed minutes after the Spartans defeated Florida for the 2000 NCAA national championship. Izzo and Cleaves shared a special bond. Izzo's adopted son's middle name is Mateen. Left: LSJ's front page joined in the celebration. *LSJ Archives*

▶ **Big Ten champs:** Net thrust skyward, MSU basketball coach Tom Izzo savors a 1999 home court victory over Wisconsin, clinching the Big Ten title. MSU went to the NCAA's Final Four that year. *LSJ Archives*

▲ **Cheers from afar:** Spartan fans who didn't have tickets to the 2000 Final Four had to content themselves with easy chairs and a TV. Here, fans set up a tent outside, furnished it with couches, and settled in to watch MSU beat Florida in the title game. *LSJ Archives*

◆ **Trophy time:** Izzo and his Spartans hoist the 2000 championship trophy. *LSJ Archives*

▸▸ **All the comforts of home:** What's a Spartan home football game without pre-game tailgating? Fans bring all the ingredients needed for a successful tailgate: Food, beverages, grills and, in this case, a comfy sofa. *LSJ Archives*

▲ **Bottom's up:** The Iowa Hawkeye's mascot turns his tail feathers to a crowd of Spartan fans who were heckling the bird during a 2003 game at Spartan Stadium. *LSJ Archives*

CHAPTER TEN

Newsmakers

D-Day. Assassination. Moon landing. Terrorist attack. They are stories we all remember – some which we'd just as soon forget.

Stories splashed across the top of a newspaper's front page often recount events that are momentous, controversial, or horrific. Life is not always pretty; sometimes it is pretty awful. That is the nature of news.

What may surprise readers of the Lansing State Journal is that, sometimes, important news and good news dance a graceful duet. They're one and the same.

The arrival of the new millennium might have been a chilling story of a world brought to a screeching halt by computer failures. Instead, our Jan. 1, 2000 front page was a compendium of worldwide celebrations. No big technology meltdowns, no big disaster.

And so it goes in this Newsmakers chapter. There are accidents and a sensational murder trial and the wrenching sight of a mother grieving for her dead son.

But herein you also will find the heartwarming story of adoption at Christmastime, a hockey game that was all about setting a world record, and a soldier home from the war, hugging his young son for the first time.

These were newsmakers, too, deserving of front-page headlines and photos. And that's what they got.

◄ **Home from Iraq:** Marine Lance Corporal Tom Christensen hugs his infant son, Tyler, for the first time. Christensen returned to Lansing in 2004 after serving in Iraq. With him is his girlfriend and Tyler's mother, Heather Barrett. *LSJ Archives*

► **Leaders, past and present:** Just days from the end of his presidency, Bill Clinton came to MSU to give the commencement address in January 2001. Here, Clinton gets an embrace from newly elected U.S. Sen. Debbie Stabenow. Stabenow, from Lansing, was elected Michigan's first female U.S. senator in 2000. *LSJ Archives*

▲ **The tide turns:** News of the D-Day invasion marked a turning point in World War II. Less than a year, and many thousands of casualties later, the war was over. *LSJ Archives*

▲ **Hiroshima bombed:** On August 6, 1945, the United States dropped a single bomb on Hiroshima. The Atomic Age had begun. *LSJ Archives*

▲ **One small step:** Apollo 11 astronauts Edwin "Buzz" Aldrin and Neil Armstrong trod lunar soil during the historic moon mission in July 1969. The moon missions had a Lansing connection: The rovers used for lunar exploration had equipment designed by Lansing's Abrams Aerial Survey Corp. *LSJ Archives*

◄ **Nov. 22, 1963:** Shots were fired, a president lay dead, and a nation fell into mourning. *LSJ Archives*

THE STATE JOURNAL
Michigan's Complete Newspaper

FRIDAY, AUGUST 9, 1974, LANSING, MICHIGAN   PRICE—15 CENTS

President Ford Takes Helm

> ". . . I am indebted to no man and only to one woman, my dear wife…"

No Immunity Arranged

President and Mrs. Gerald Ford after ceremony

Tearful Nixon Flies Home to California

President Ford Asks Nation To Pray for Him, Nixon

Ford Can't Run Twice

Inside the Journal

▲ **Surrogate controversy:** Surrogate births via artificial insemination were new to the world in 1983, when Lansing's Judy Stiver agreed to bear the child of a New York man for $10,000. The infant, at first known only as "Baby Doe", had a birth defect and became the focal point of a nationally renowned controversy. New York accountant Alexander Mahaloff claimed not to be the child's father, a fact borne out by blood tests. The case prompted state laws regulating surrogate arrangements. Judy and Ray Stiver decided to keep the brain-damaged child. Christopher Ray Stiver turned 21 in 2004. *LSJ Archives*

◄ **Commander in chief:** Grand Rapids' Gerald R. Ford became the 38th president in 1974, when Richard Nixon resigned in the wake of the Watergate scandal. Ford later pardoned Nixon, which likely contributed to his 1976 election defeat. Ford is the only president to come from Michigan. *LSJ Archives*

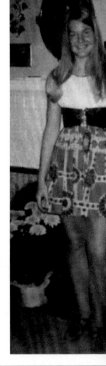

▶ **Mayor's daughter kidnapped:** Laurie Murninghan, the 16-year-old daughter of Lansing Mayor Max Murninghan, was kidnapped by a gunman on July 9, 1970. Her body was found 11 days later in a wooded area southeast of Lansing. She had been strangled. Her killer was never caught, though police re-examined the case using new technology. Her murder is still unsolved. *LSJ Archives*

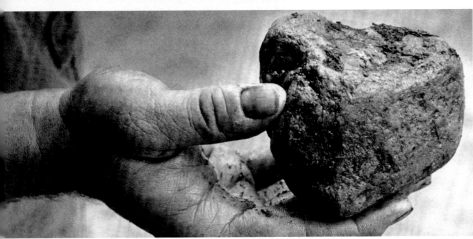

◀ ▼ ▶ Elephant emergency:
A team of veterinary surgeons perform an operation on Potter Park Zoo's "Bingo" the elephant in 1979. Someone had thrown a rock into Bingo's pen, which Bingo picked up and attempted to swallow. The rock became lodged in the elephant's throat. Though surgeons successfully removed the rock (below), infection later set in and Bingo died. It was a sad day for Lansing schoolchildren, who had collected thousands of dollars to help bring Bingo to the zoo. *Courtesy Norris Ingells*

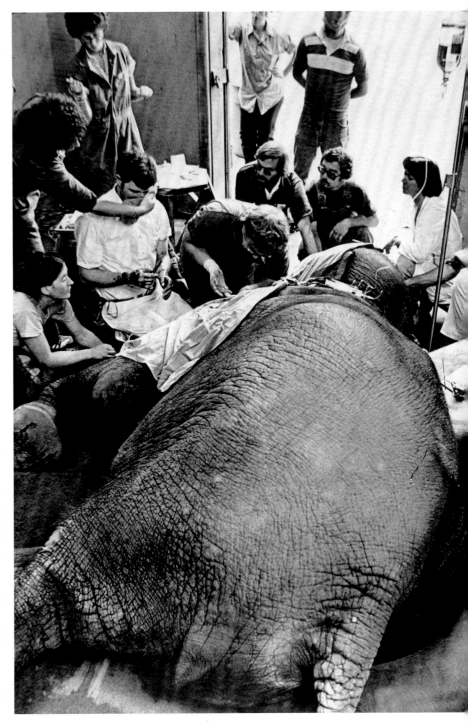

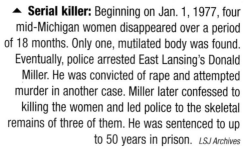

▲ **Serial killer:** Beginning on Jan. 1, 1977, four mid-Michigan women disappeared over a period of 18 months. Only one, mutilated body was found. Eventually, police arrested East Lansing's Donald Miller. He was convicted of rape and attempted murder in another case. Miller later confessed to killing the women and led police to the skeletal remains of three of them. He was sentenced to up to 50 years in prison. *LSJ Archives*

▶ **Francine Hughes:** The 30-year-old Dansville mother of four was acquitted in 1977 of killing her abusive husband. Hughes admitted to setting fire to the bed he was sleeping in. The jury found her not guilty by reason of temporary insanity. Hughes' story inspired a 1984 movie, "The Burning Bed", starring Farrah Fawcett. The case also inspired the song "Independence Day" by country singer Martina McBride. *LSJ Archives*

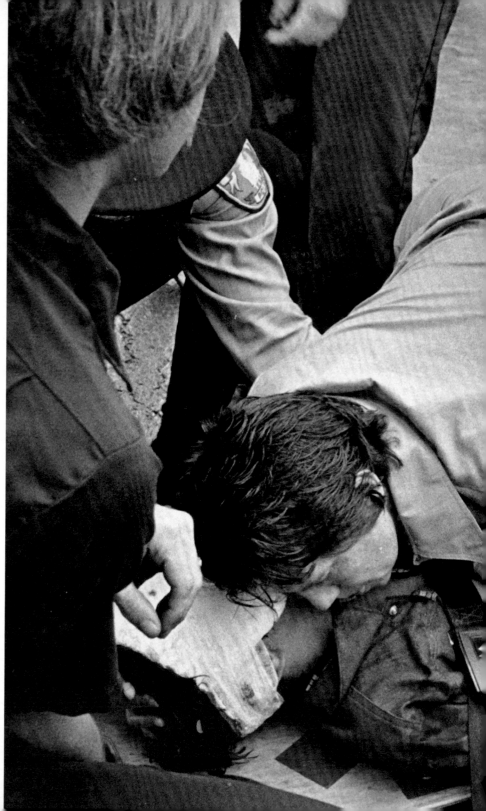

◀ **1977 Skywalk accident:**
A mother comforts her injured child, one of six children hurt when the boom of a 40-ton crane slammed into a skywalk near Barnes Avenue School. "It was a nightmare," one witness said. The six children were hospitalized. All eventually recovered. *Courtesy Norris Ingells*

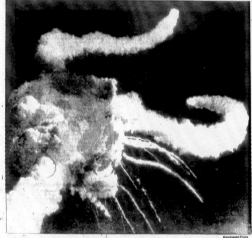

▲ **It's a tradition:** Since 1986, Ingham County Probate Judge George Economy has presided over a happy occasion on or near each Christmas Eve. Economy formally signs adoption papers, legally creating new families. In this 1997 photo, the judge lets Ashley and Marcus Keys lower the gavel to make their adoption final. *LSJ Archives*

◀ **Shuttle disaster:** A scene etched in the minds of many Americans, the space shuttle Challenger explodes just two minutes into flight. The 1986 disaster killed the seven astronauts aboard, including teacher Christa McAuliffe. Faulty O rings in the solid rocket booster were eventually blamed for the accident. *LSJ Archives*

▶ **Two presidents:** Former U.S. president and Michigan congressman Gerald R. Ford (left) attended the 1998 dedication ceremonies of the Detroit College of Law at MSU. With him is MSU President Peter McPherson. *LSJ Archives*

▲ **Return to MSU:** President Bill Clinton congratulates MSU graduates at the 1995 commencement ceremonies. Clinton was on campus in 1992 for the televised debates with then-President George Bush and third-party candidate Ross Perot. *LSJ Archives*

▲ **Oldsmobile centennial:** In celebration of Oldsmobile's 100th birthday, Olds owners from around the world descended on Lansing in August 1997. An hours-long parade down Michigan Avenue was the highlight. The parade had at least one Oldsmobile representing every year of production. Some owners of the vintage cars drove their vehicles across the country to attend. *LSJ Archives*

◀ **It's Christmastime in the city:** Lansing's annual Silver Bells in the City finishes with a bang. The state Capitol's Christmas tree is lit, followed by star bursts of fireworks behind the lighted Capitol dome. More than 50,000 people attend the downtown's annual pre-Thanksgiving event. *LSJ Archives*

Riots: In March 1999, more than 5,000 people amassed in East Lansing streets following an MSU loss in the NCAA basketball tournament's Final Four. Students and nonstudents alike started fires and vandalized property, causing nearly $240,000 in damage. More than 130 people were eventually arraigned on charges, half of them MSU students. This and other MSU disturbances prompted a state law that allows judges to expel students for up to two years if they're convicted of riot-related offenses. *LSJ Archives*

Lansing State Journal

www.lansingstatejournal.com

Saturday
January 1, 2000
50¢

Plaxico Burress plays last game with Spartans, headed for NFL. Details inside GAMEDAY

Welcome, 2000

World celebrates, breathes sigh of relief over Y2K

Lansing area greets 'symbolic moment'

Lansing State Journal

Six-year-old Timmy Embury rubbed the sleep from his eyes and welcomed the new millennium today — with peace, promise and electrical power.

As midnight passed, the Morrice boy slept through the initial wave of fireworks and more than 500 blaring car horns at Lansing's Ranney Park.

The dreaded Y2K computer bug passed into history with barely a sputter. As 2000 dawned, no significant computer glitches were reported by Lansing area governments, hospitals or utility companies.

However, the state's Year 2000 Project Office Web site dedicated to getting Michigan into the 21st century read early today that Michigan still had 364 days, 23 hours and minutes to go before the year 2000.

And so the future began with a new day, new year, new century and new millennium.

"We need to learn from our history — so we can build a better future," Timmy's father, Tim, said moments before waking the boy — who slept in the front seat of a red Ford pickup as the party began. "This is a symbolic moment."

And it went without any major problems.

"It was a dead bug," said Charles Routh, operations chief at the Emergency Coordination Center.

Dispatchers at the Lansing 911 Center dealt with rowdy party revelers at midnight — not computer glitches. The biggest problems were overzealous celebrators shooting off guns to welcome the new year and a fire in Michigan State University's Agriculture Hall. No one was injured in the fire.

Lansing's estimated, 911 systems, power lines and city sewer systems worked fine.

With the exception of a switching error that knocked out power to about 2,800 Lansing area homes for 40 seconds at 9:03 p.m., Lansing's Board of Water and Light laced little difficulty.

While no Y2K problems were apparent, an official from the Federal Emergency Management Agency said mid-Michigan will have to wait until Monday before the full effects of the Y2K computer bug are known.

"We'll see how well those smaller entities prepared. Monday will be the telling," said Jeanne Millin, Michigan liaison for the federal agency, who will remain in Lansing through the weekend.

This night will go down in

Please see NEW YEAR, 15A

Conserving power
The Lansing Board of Water and Light reduced electricity to other Midwest companies. The move helped prevent an outage.

Sail drops: Times Square celebrated New Year's Eve for the world in a wild street party that erupted when

Ushering in 2000 around the globe

Lansing

Washington, D.C.

Madrid, Spain

Inside
- World embraces dawn of new millennium with lights, fireworks. Page 16A
- Did you survive Y2K? Take this quiz and find out. Page 1D

the millennium arrived in the United States. More than a million people packed the square.

KATHY WILLENS/Associated Press

Across THE WORLD

World marks start of new age

Associated Press

Millions joyously packed the city streets of Europe and the Americas to join in a worldwide welcome for the new millennium, ignoring fears of terrorist attack and computer collapse to revel in a shimmering spectacle of song, light and fireworks.

From South Sea islands to the southernmost city in the world, from the Eiffel Tower to New York's Times Square, they partied and prayed for a better world.

The pop of a huge crystal ball in Times Square, a ritual almost as old as the century, set off an explosion of fireworks, cheering and tears as the millennium came to the U.S. mainland.

Also in New York City, a Michigan man accused of illegally carrying a weapon in was arrested Friday.

About 6 p.m., detectives noticed a man carrying handcuffs at a parking garage on 53rd Street, and after approaching him, spotted a shotgun in plain view inside the vehicle. The man, identified as George James, 29, of Saranac was arrested and charged with criminal possession of a weapon. The gun was loaded and uncensed, police said.

More than 1 million people packed Times Square, "crossroads of the world," for the biggest, splashiest American celebration, guarded by 8,000 police.

Woven together by satellite TV, the world's nearly 200 countries, in their 24 time zones, became a jamboree of disparate cultures — South Pacific islanders singing Handel's "Hallelujah" chorus, Buddhist monks praying for peace in Japan, a German choir singing in a church in Nazareth, Israel, and a huge French-made bell tolling a welcome in Newport, R.I., for each time zone entering 2000.

Fireworks lighted up the skies over Sydney, Australia, and over Rome, where Pope John Paul II gave thanks for humanity's triumphs and asked forgiveness for its sins.

In Washington, President

Please see 2000, 15A

Across the MILLENNIA

From a Y2K-inspired gas fillup at 12:45 a.m. to downtown parties at midnight, Mid-Michigan prepared for the promise of a new millennium

Pages 16A-13A

Special keepsake section for the new millennium
A 28-page section looks ahead to the 21st century. Inside

With humanity intact, let's strive for change

So, now what are you going to do with all that Spam? How are you going to use up that bottled water and freeze-dried lasagna?

Here's an idea: a party, a bash to celebrate our passage from, the realm of the nines to the realm of the zeros. Maybe it wasn't a flawless passage. Maybe be a computer here or there tried uncle. Maybe we were inconvenienced.

But we're conscious by this is no time to quibble over whether today is the first day of the first year of a new millennium or the first day of the last year of an old one.

We can all agree on this: Today, as we count our fingers and toes and realize that we have not been devoured, after the apocalypse bug, we blink our bleary eyes at an outer-

inspiring string of goose eggs. 2-0-0-0.

Oh, boy. It's better than Square One. It's Square Zero—the freshest of fresh starts. And with our planet occupying its customary niche in the universe — with our own skin cooking and our noses still posed to represent.

This modern erosion of compassion for those of us who can't make it on our own? Blame or us. But let's not waste time regretting it; let's just fix it.

A major renovation? Oh, that's just the first phase. Wait until you see the completed list. The important thing is that we're alive, present and accounted for. Our toehold in the cosmos may be as tenuous as ever, but it's a toehold, nonetheless.

This growing joy — particularly in the United States — between the haves and the have-nots? It's not good for the poor. It's poison for democracy — and just about everything that America is supposed to be.

— take Sunday off. We'll get Named Monday bright and early.

Doing what? Well, I've been so blithely intent for a bit of progress — asking some fellow earthlings where they thought the remodeling should begin. Here, in no particular order, is what they told me:

This practice of killing each other as a way of resolving conflict? It's so ... yesterday. Surely we're better than that.

This tendency to assign human value on the basis of skin color? Come on, people — have we been thinking? Surely we're ready to move past that.

2-0-0-0: one more chance to do it right.

What do you think? Call John Schneider at 377-1179, send a fax to 377-1299, or e-mail jschneid@lansing.gannett.com. Include your name, telephone number, city, town or township. John's column runs daily.

Inside

Local B   Sports C
Today D   Classified F

Advertiser Index 2A
Ann Landers 9C
Business/Stocks 9C
Crossword/Comics ...8C
Deaths 2B
Lottery 2B

FestEve
About 7,000 people watched fireworks at Ranney Park, which wrapped up an evening of alcohol-free activities.

Gas prices
The price of gasoline rose about 15 cents per gallon over two days along Cedar Street. Year's Eve price: $1.20.

Groceries
Customers lingered at empty shelves all day as stores struggled to keep up with the demand for bottled water.

Emergency workers
The Lansing 911 staff dealt mainly with fireworks complaints and overzealous partiers, not computer glitches.

▲ **GM stays:** A spirited "Keep GM" campaign, led by Lansing Mayor David Hollister (right), paid off in 2002 when General Motors opened a new assembly plant in Lansing. With Hollister is GM President and CEO Rick Wagoner. Lansing officials feared that the phasing out of an old assembly plant might prompt GM to leave Lansing altogether. With coaxing, and state incentives, GM chose to build the Grand River Assembly Plant, which produces Cadillacs. Early in 2004, GM also began building a new assembly plant in Delta Township. *LSJ Archives*

◀ **All Y2K:** For a time, Y2K was the world's buzzword. Shorthand for "Year 2000," it signaled the beginning of a new millennium – as well as the potential for calamity. Would computers work? Would panic and havoc ensue? As it happened, little happened. The world celebrated, tidied up and carried on. *LSJ Archives*

◀ **Record on ice:** On Oct. 6, 2001, MSU's hockey team entered a strange arena – Spartan Stadium. They called it the "Cold War," but the real goal was to set a world record. They did. MSU played the University of Michigan team before 74,554 fans – a world record for a hockey crowd. The game ended in a 3-3 tie. *LSJ Archives*

▶ **Call to arms:** Mason resident Ron Smith gives a goodbye hug to his mom, Cathy Damon. Smith was called active duty in the Marine Corps in 2003, as the Iraq war got under way. *LSJ Archives*

◀ ▼ **In memory:** After 13 years of arm-twisting and fundraising, Michigan got its own Vietnam monument. Dedicated in 2001, the $3.4 million project was spearheaded by the United Auto Workers and various state motorcycle clubs. The 120-foot-long steel arc lists the names of the 2,654 people from Michigan who died in the Vietnam War. Left: Veterans and their families sing "God Bless America" and applaud the monument's dedication. *LSJ Archives*

▲ **A mother's grief:** Apolonia Rosas clutches the flag from her son's casket during a 2004 funeral in Lansing. PFC Richard "Ricky" Rosas was killed by a roadside bomb in Iraq. As of September 2004, more than 1,000 U.S. troops had died in that country. *LSJ Archives*

THE STATE REPUBLICAN.

DARIUS D. THORP,
LAW PUBLISHER,
PRINTING & BINDING

CHAPTER ELEVEN

LSJ, Past & Present

The man who created what became the Lansing State Journal deserves a lengthy chapter of his own. Here, suffice it to say that Henry Barns was a bit of an adventurer, a politician, and a businessman through and through. After several forays into the publishing world, Barns – one of the founders of the Republican Party – decided Michigan's capital city needed a newspaper with a Republican agenda.

Barns arrived with his printing press on April 24, 1855. Four days later, on April 28, the first edition of the weekly Lansing Republican was published. (Yearly subscriptions in those days were as low as $1.) This first newspaper office, a low-slung log cabin, was located at the corner of Washington Avenue and Ionia Street.

Though meant chiefly as a propaganda machine for the Michigan Republican Party, the newspaper also soaked up tabloid tidbits from around the country. One of its first issues reported how a Baltimore woman had lost her child in a poker game.

The newspaper underwent many name changes during the next several decades. In 1911, it became the State Journal upon merging with another daily newspaper. The newspaper offices also moved locations several times, but always in or close to downtown Lansing. In 1951, the State Journal moved to its present headquarters, 120 E. Lenawee St. in downtown Lansing. In 1994, LSJ opened its production facility in Delta Township.

Over the past 150 years, our reporters and photographers have witnessed extraordinary events and breathtaking change. Changes at LSJ have been no less extraordinary. News stories that once were painstakingly typed on lead "slugs" and set by hand to make printing plates are, today, electronically beamed from a computer to our Delta Township printing plant.

Some things, however, never change in the news-gathering business. Reporters and photographers still "dig" for stories. Editors edit them. When the paper is "put to bed," 24 tons of newsprint roll through the presses to create the daily edition.

And by early the next morning, before most of us have had our first sip of coffee, the LSJ has reached its final destination – some 163,000 readers every day.

Henry Barns

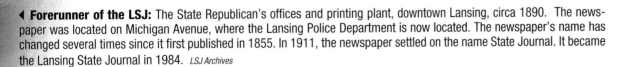

◀ **Forerunner of the LSJ:** The State Republican's offices and printing plant, downtown Lansing, circa 1890. The newspaper was located on Michigan Avenue, where the Lansing Police Department is now located. The newspaper's name has changed several times since it first published in 1855. In 1911, the newspaper settled on the name State Journal. It became the Lansing State Journal in 1984. *LSJ Archives*

▶ **New location:** In the early part of the 20th century, the State Journal offices were located in at 230 N. Washington Ave. In 1914, the newspaper moved its operations to 202 N. Grand Ave., where it remained until 1951, when it moved to its present location, 120 E. Lenawee St. The building at right later became Benson's Hardware. *LSJ Archives*

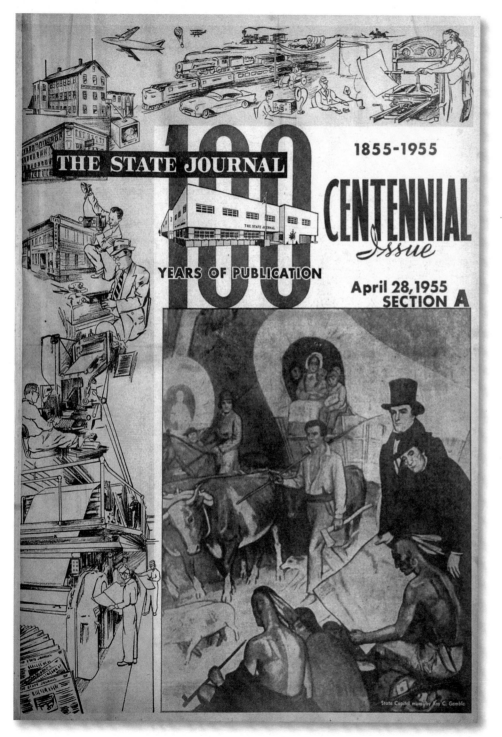

◀ ▲ **100-year anniversary:** On April 28, 1955, the Lansing State Journal published a special 336-page edition commemorating its centennial year. It was a history of Lansing, among other things, and took more than a year to research, write and produce. It included a congratulatory letter from President Dwight D. Eisenhower. Above: The cover of the "Press and People" section of the centennial edition, depicting the various buildings that quartered the State Journal through the years. *LSJ Archives*

▲ **Some things don't change:** LSJ still depends on people to deliver its daily product. Most of today's carriers, however, are adults. In the 1920s, when this photo was taken, the State Journal's army of carriers had a decidedly youthful look. *LSJ Archives*

▼ **Cornerstone readied:** A work crew sets the cornerstone in place for the new State Journal building. A time capsule was placed inside the cornerstone during the 1951 dedication. Fifty-three years later, LSJ's news and business operations remain at 120 E. Lenawee St. *LSJ Archives*

▲ **Linotype era:** For decades, most newspaper stories were painstakingly compiled on Linotype machines. Linotype operators typed in reporters' "copy" on the Linotypes, which produced full lines of type made out of lead "slugs." This Linotype, and dozens more like it at LSJ, were phased out of use in the late 1970s. *LSJ Archives*

◄ **Next step:** After a full page of Linotype-produced stories was done, it was assembled on a "chase", a heavy metal frame which could lock in the type so it wouldn't shift. This became the basis for a printing plate. *LSJ Archives*

◀ **Our downtown headquarters:** The State Journal moved into its new digs in 1951. It remains today at 120 E. Lenawee St., in downtown Lansing. LSJ's printing operations are located in Delta Township. In 1984, the newspaper became the Lansing State Journal. *LSJ Archives*

▶ **Creating a news page:** Copy editors Cathy Bacile and Don Pepper are two of several editors who "build" news pages on their computer screens. In a process called "paginating," news stories, photos and headlines are assembled on one page. Advertisements are placed on pages by a separate department. Once an entire page is complete, it is electronically transmitted to LSJ's printing plant in Delta Township, where a printing plate is made. The page is then affixed to the printing press. *LSJ Archives*

◀ **Press check:** LSJ press operator John Marshall makes a quality-control check during a press run of an August 2004 edition. The State Journal's printing operations moved from 120 E. Lenawee St. to the current Delta Township site in 1994. LSJ's news, advertising and circulation operations remain on Lenawee Street in downtown Lansing.

LSJ Archives

Getting the story: Longtime LSJ reporter Hugh Leach interviews Lansing's Casey Moubray for a story on the Michigan Senior Olympics in August 2004. Leach is one of 21 LSJ reporters in a newsroom of 66 people.

LSJ Archives

What a year: 2003 was a year of war, worry, and various natural or man-made calamities. In other words, a typical lap around the sun for planet Earth. *LSJ Archives*

Pictures tell a story: LSJ photographer Becky Shink focuses on her subject for a 2004 assignment. Shink is one of four award-winning photographers at the State Journal. *LSJ Archives*

Ready to read: 72,000 copies of the Lansing State Journal land on doorsteps and in news racks each weekday. LSJ is read by 163,000 people every day.

LSJ Archives

Sunday
DECEMBER 28, 2003

Lansing State Journal

Rain showers
HIGH IN THE UPPER 40s,
Page 6B

$1.50

www.lsj.com

YEAR IN REVIEW 2003

War, shuttle tragedy, blackout are top stories of tumultuous year

January 2, 2003

February 2, 2003

February 9, 2003

March 20, 2003

March 24, 2003

April 10, 2003

April 13, 2003

May 4, 2003

August 15, 2003

September 28, 2003

December 14, 2003

December 15, 2003